This book is dedicated to
Dr Colin S. Millar OBE
16 Sept 1937 – 22 July 2019
A tireless worker on all matters concerning Bennachie

Published by

the Bailies of Bennachie
www.bailiesofbennachie.co.uk

ISBN 978-0-9576384-2-6

Cover picture: courtesy of Christine Foster
Many thanks to Sue Taylor for proof-reading and editorial suggestions

Printed by
MMS-Almac Ltd., Unit 4-6, Tyock Industrial Estate, Elgin

Typesetting, layout and graphics reproduction by Colin Shepherd

CONTENTS

The Bailies of Bennachie

A POSSIBLE BEACH OF A GLACIAL LAKE ON THE HILL OF TILLYMORGAN, ABERDEENSHIRE

Andrew Wainwright

INTRODUCTION

Layers of gravel were seen in trenches on the higher slopes of Hill of Tillymorgan which are interpreted as the beaches of a large lake covering the Insch and Huntly valleys. If accepted as such they would provide additional evidence that this area of North-east Scotland was ice-free during part of the last glaciation.

Wind turbines were installed on the Hill of Tillymorgan in 2016 and, in the trench for the electric cables, a thin layer of gravel was observed, by chance, as the author was walking past to visit the slate quarries at the top of the hill. This layer is about 50cms thick with the upper surface merging with the overlying drift and with a sharp lower contact to underlying sediments. It can be followed for about 10m into the hillside where the base rises and where, eventually, the gravel pinches out (see Photo 1 and Figure 1). It occurs at an elevation of 240m above present day mean sea level (amsl.) at NGR NJ 649 336. A thicker section of similar material was seen further up the track in a small temporary quarry at an approximate elevation of 254 - 256m amsl. Still further up the track towards the turbines more gravel was seen but could not be examined before the trench was filled in. The highest gravel seen was at approximately 240m. Again, below 240m the presence or absence of gravel could not be ascertained because the trench had been backfilled before the site was first seen.

Photo 1. Gravel at 240amsl in side of trench (level is 1m long). Hillside slopes down to the left and gravel pinches out to the right.

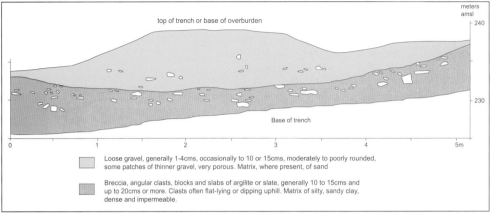

Figure 1. Section drawing of trench.

NATURE OF THE GRAVEL AT 240m

The gravel at 240m amsl was examined closely and sampled. Photo 2 shows how clean and well-sorted this material is. It overlies (just below the ruler) a very different sediment which is a breccia made up of angular fragments of slate in a muddy matrix. On first sight before the section was cleaned up the contact was very apparent because a considerable amount of water was seeping out of the bottom of the gravel over the underlying breccia.

Photo 2. Close-up of gravel showing the well-sorted beach gravel overlying the ill-sorted and angular breccia underneath.

The gravel consists of clasts (individual pebbles) of slate and argillite and is very well sorted. Almost all of the clasts are between 10mm and 40mm in diameter with very few bigger than 50mm and none seen above 100mm (see Grain Size Analysis, Figure 2). The clasts would be described as rounded or subrounded (all corners and most faces have been smoothed by abrasion in water), but the very largest and smallest ones tend to be more angular. The small amount of matrix present consists of sand, silt, and mud. The sand is mainly small fragments of slate; no quartz sand was seen.

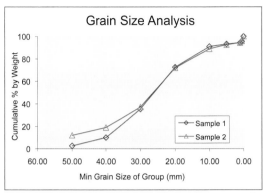

Figure 2. Grain size analysis. See text for explanation.)

The grain size analysis (Figure 2) presents the cumulative percentage of the material by weight plotted against the minimum grain size for that fraction. Thus, for both samples, almost 90% of the material has a grain size greater than 10mm, so that for both samples, less than 10% of the material is smaller than this size. Similarly, material larger than 40mm represents 20% of sample 2 but only 10% of sample 1. The steepness of the curves shows that the samples are well sorted. A well-sorted sand typically has a void space of about 30%. The fact that only 10% of this material is less than 10mm means that the spaces between the clasts will be largely empty. As a result the gravel is very permeable and, in the trench, water was seeping out along its lower surface keeping the underlying breccia wet.

The underlying material is very different. It is a breccia, which means that it consists of angular clasts (the corners are still sharp) in a matrix of clay, silt and sand. Clasts are of all sizes up to 20 or 25cms and made of slate and other argillites. They are of the same material as those in the gravel but are of completely different shapes. Also, the void spaces are totally packed with matrix that makes it largely impermeable.

Local Geology

The maps published by the British Geological Survey show the hill above the site is composed of slates of the Hill of Foudland Pelite member composed of metamorphosed mudstones and silty mudstones. Below the site the Macduff Formation comes in and this is composed of metamorphosed muddy sandstones and siltstones. They are both part of the Dalradian Series and date from about 1000 to 541 million years ago. At the bottom of the hill and across most of the Insch valley various members of the Insch Pluton occur. These are basic and ultra basic rocks intruded between 485.4 and 443.8 million years ago during the Ordovician period.

The Hill of Foudland Pelite member is the material found in the slate quarries at the top of the Hill of Tillymorgan and along the hills to the west as far as the River Bogie and a bit beyond. The Macduff Formation is too coarse and sandy to form slates and this is why the quarries are only found at the tops of the hills and down the north sides.

Over most of the area exposure is poor. The area is covered by young surface sediments which the British Geological Survey describe as 'diamictite'. This term covers a mixture of mud, silt, sand, and larger fragments of rock, all mixed together with little internal structure. Diamictite is usually ascribed a glacial origin and can include glacial till (the material left behind by glaciers) and solifluxion deposits (formed by down-slope movement of material by a continuous freeze/thaw action).

INTERPRETATION OF SEDIMENTS

Both the gravel and the breccia were deposited during the Pleistocene glacial period (2 million to 10 thousand years ago). This was a time of long and extremely cold winters with brief, warm summers. The prevailing wind direction was from the west or south-west and so the bulk of the precipitation would have fallen over the western hills and as far east as the Cairngorms. Also, easterly winds which now bring snow to the northeast would not have blown over open sea but over ice, so would not have picked up much moisture. Therefore, in the west, precipitation of snow would have been sufficient to overcome summer melting and great thickness of ice and glaciers built up. However, further east winter snowfall would not have been deep enough to survive the warm summers and no ice would have accumulated. With the lack of snow and ice to provide insulation, the ground would have been completely frozen for several hundred meters and so would have been totally impermeable. In summer only the surface would have melted. The melt water being unable to soak away would have turned the surface sediments to mud, which would have flowed slowly downhill under gravity. Under these conditions the resulting sediments were completely mixed and now look like they had been put through a cement mixer. It typically filled-in hollows and rounded off bumps producing smooth, gentle concave slopes. This is referred to as solifluxion and is one of many periglacial processes. It is also commonly the origin of diamictite.

The breccia formed under these annual freeze/thaw cycles under permafrost conditions. Significant movement by water, whether in a river or on a beach, can be discounted because of the lack of sorting, the angularity of the clasts and the presence of matrix filling all the available void space.

The origin of the gravel is more difficult to identify, particularly in view of its elevation at 240m amsl. However, the rounded nature of the clasts and the relative lack of fine grained material would imply steady movement by water in a back and forth manner with a nearby area of deeper water where the fine grained material could end up. The lack of any cross-bedding or other sedimentary structures would imply that the water movement was not in one direction only, but occurred in an oscillating manner. These conditions would not be satisfied by deposition from a river but would be consistent with constant reworking on a beach.

The outline of the lake related to this beach can be seen on Figure 3 where the 250m contour has been highlighted. It would have extended to Bennachie in the south and as far west as Rhynie and the Cabrach. At this elevation it would have extended through both the Glens of Foudland and the valley of the Bogie and so to the area around Huntly and beyond. Note that there are no hills above this elevation to either the north or the east.

The location of this gravel at an elevation of 240m with nothing to the north or east to dam it up is a problem and has to be explained. During the Pleistocene period, continental ice sheets moved out of northern Europe into the North Sea, and at the same time ice flowed from the Spey Valley and the Great Glen through the Moray Firth. As a result the Moray Firth and the North Sea were filled with ice that may have been at least a kilometre thick extending at least to the latitude of Caithness. This could well have provided the eastern and northern limits of the proposed lake

To prove the presence of a lake of this extent needs further evidence of beaches or other features at the same or very similar elevations around its proposed shore line. At the same time as the wind turbines were being built, a gas pipeline was being installed through the valley of Jericho to the west of the A96. Unfortunately this was dug, the pipe installed and the trench back-filled before it could be examined. Hopefully, this pipe will be taken down the north side of the hill in the near future permitting the trench to be examined there.

This beach material is not exposed and cannot be seen at the ground surface. To explain this it is proposed that after the lake drained, freezing conditions continued and any surface manifestation of the beaches were removed by solifluxion processes. In the adjacent field to the south east of the site there is a steep slope at a similar level which may have been a small cliff behind an equivalent beach. Similar features can be seen elsewhere in the Insch valley at a similar elevation; they are not often seen at other elevations. Further exposures of similar beach gravels are likely to be seen only in trenches dug by farmers for drainage work.

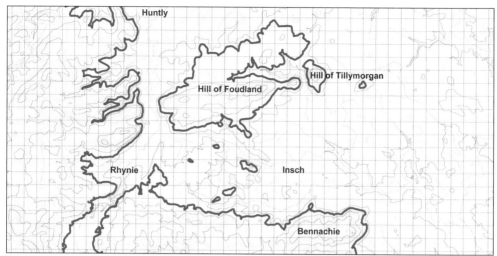

Figure 3. Topography from Bennachie in the south to Huntly in the North showing the 250m contour - the approximate line of the proposed beach.

Beaches formed along the edges of glacial lakes are found elsewhere in Scotland. The most famous being the 'Parallel Roads' of Glen Roy. (There is a good visitor site in this glen, the waters of which flow into Glen Spean not far to the east of Fort William.) Here, ice in the Great Glen dammed a lake in Glen Roy that spilled over a series of passes into neighbouring glens. In this instance, the spillways were set in rock, and so the lake level stayed the same for some time. As a result, the beaches are more substantial than the example considered here and can clearly be seen on the neighbouring hillsides.

THE SIGNIFICANCE OF THIS POSSIBLE BEACH

The discussion of whether the North East of Scotland was ice-covered during the last glaciation has gone on since the earliest studies of the region. The arguments were summarised by Clapperton and Sugden (1975) and more recently by Merritt and Leslie (2009). Indisputable glacial tills are found along the coast all around North-east Scotland. From Aberdeen to Peterhead it is red in colour, being derived from ice flowing out from Glenmore over the Old Red Sandstone there. From Peterhead to Fraserburgh and in patches further west along the Moray Firth, it is blue/grey when fresh. It clearly flowed over the Moray Firth as it contains blocks of fosiliferous Jurrassic and Cretaceous rocks and has been proven to exist there by oil drilling. The ice from which these deposits came probably resided in the Great Glen and the Spey Valley. Both these tills are found close to the coast and sometimes appear to have been pushed up over the land from the seaward side. Neither of them are found far inland. It is suggested that ice flowing out from Scandinavia and Northern Europe deflected the ice flowing out from Scotland. This idea is supported by the presence of glacial erratics of Norwegian rocks being found in gravels along the coast.

Arguing for ice-cover over the area, Merritt and Leslie refer to the presence of meltwater channels which were formed by water flowing under glaciers. However, the examples they quote are all close to the coast. They do not refer specifically to any further west than Turriff.

In favour of the lack of ice, Synge (1956) used the presence of tors on Bennachie, rotted bedrock (e.g. the quarry of rotted granite at the Rowan Tree car park, Bennachie) and weathered till. He also argued that the smooth hillsides seen in the area are the result of periglacial processes and not glacial action, which would be expected to leave a more irregular profile with hard rocks protruding.

Against this they all maintain that if the area was ice-free, there should be signs of the presence of large ice-dammed lakes. If present these would have led to the formation of lake-bottom sediments, deltas and beach deposits, none of which they claim to have seen. Thus, if the gravels at 240m, and those seen briefly at higher elevations are accepted as beach deposits, the arguments for an ice-free area in North-east Scotland are strengthened.

References

Blair, J.	2017	The Parallel Roads of Glen Roy, Lochaber: Unlocking the Lines in the Landscape. www.scottishgeology.com/best-places/parallel-roads-glen-roy
Clapperton, C.M. and Sugden, D.E.	1975	*"The Glaciation of Buchan:- a reappraisal"*, in Quaternary Studies in North East Scotland, Ed. Gemmel, A.M.D.
Merritt, J. & Leslie, G.	2009	Northeast Scotland, a Landscape Fashioned by Geology, Scottish Natural Heritage, Redgorton.
Synge, F.M.	1956	*"The Glaciation of North East Scotland"*, in Scottish Geographical Magazine, 712, 129-143.

PRELIMINARY SURVEY OF THE MOTH POPULATION ON BENNACHIE

David Hood

INTRODUCTION

It is perhaps surprising to discover there are over 500 species of larger moths, known as macro-moths, in Scotland and over 900 micro-moths. Many are frankly spectacular, and even the more modest species have remarkably subtle and attractive colouration and patterning. This has evolved to improve their survival chances in their own particular habitat. The Bennachie plateau and its surroundings offer a significant range of habitat types, and would be expected to have a reasonable variety of moth species. This report summarizes the results of trapping sessions, carried out mainly around the eastern end of Bennachie during 2018. During this process 142 species of moths were identified.

There is a network of enthusiasts across the country who report their moth sightings to a local County Moth Recorder. After verifying reports, the Recorder enters them into a national database - the National Moth Recording Scheme (NMRS). The NMRS is run by Butterfly Conservation (BC) who hold national statistics on moth populations. Trends in populations of different moth species are regarded as sensitive indicators of issues such as habitat loss and climate change. Data from the NMRS is used to inform such research. BC is shortly to publish the Atlas of Britain and Ireland's Larger Moths showing distributions of all British Isles macro-moths. Much of the recent data used for these maps has come from moth recorders monitoring their local moth populations.

Today, moths are generally recorded as photos rather than the killed specimens kept by collectors in Victorian times and the early 20th century. Traps use a light source, generally some type of UV light, to attract the moths which then enter through a funnel, or similar structure, into a holding chamber. To encourage them to settle, egg boxes are put in the chamber and the moths usually creep under these and hide in the cavities. Presumably this mimics their usual daytime resting places. The trap can be monitored during the course of an evening, or the light may be left on overnight and the moths checked in the morning. Once the moths have been identified they are released unharmed.

Left: Mains-powered trap; Right: A trial portable LED trap.

Where there is access to mains electricity, it is simplest to use this to power the light trap. However, this limits the locations which can be surveyed. Traps have been used in more isolated locations powered by 12V car batteries (very heavy) or by portable generators (even heavier!). The weight limitations make it difficult to use these traps very far from a road. Consequently, in order to survey moths on the Bennachie plateau, a lighter trap suitable for transporting on foot or bicycle, was trialled. This trap, using LEDs as a light source, permitted the use of a lightweight battery. A French-designed moth trap, utilising a cage of white netting, was found to be lighter than traditional traps.

THE PRELIMINARY BENNACHIE MOTH SURVEY

Most of the trapping sessions were carried out using mains powered traps in a garden at the base of the hill, near the Bennachie Centre. Three sessions were carried out using a traditional portable trap near to Rowantree, and by the Linn Burn. The LED trap was used on the plateau between Mither Tap and Oxen Craig on three occasions to sample the species at a higher altitude.[1] In total, 26 sessions were carried out between April 11th and Oct 20th 2018.

Results of the Preliminary Survey

A wide variety of moths were caught, many of which were quite striking and beautiful. A sample of these is shown in the following photographs. The detailed results are then presented in a table which shows the total numbers of moths trapped and in which weeks they were seen. There then follows data on the frequency with which the various species were trapped, and a diagrammatic illustration of the concept of moths' flight seasons. The last section of this article describes inferences which can be drawn from the data in the table, and a selection of species with interesting stories.

Emperor Moth

A large and spectacular moth which is regarded as common on heath and moorland. The male flies by day during April and May, so why is it so rarely noticed by hill walkers? The caterpillar grows to over 6 cms, and, in its later stages is bright green with black and yellow spots, and is well camouflaged among young heather shoots. However, the author's uncle, who was red-green colour blind, could spot the caterpillars at a distance. It seemed the camouflage did not work for him!

---

1 *The trap ratings were Mains - MV 125w and Actinic 22w (10 sessions with each). Traditional portable 40w, LED portable 21w*

Elephant Hawk-moth

These moths are wonderfully camouflaged when on their main food plant, Rosebay Willowherb. This specimen was vibrating his wings to warm up his flight muscles and, shortly after the photo was taken, he was off.

Coxcomb Prominent

The Coxcomb Prominent has projections on the edge of its wings which are raised over its back when at rest giving it a distinct profile. Presumably this helps to break up the moth's outline and aids its camouflage when at rest on tree bark and among dead leaves.

Buff Tip

Common in woodland and gardens, this moth does a convincing imitation of a broken birch twig when at rest.

Brown Silver-line

Although it may fit the stereotype of dull brown moth, the Brown Silver-line is actually quite attractive. The caterpillars feed exclusively on bracken so the moth is present throughout the British Isles.

White Ermine

While White Ermine were caught on Bennachie, the example in the photo was actually trapped in France.

Burnished Brass

This moth is well named possessing shiny, metallic patches on its forewings.

Poplar Hawk-moth

This is the most common and widespread of the Hawk-moth family and occurs wherever its food plants, mainly poplars and willows, are established. It has a unique resting posture presumably to disguise its moth shape from predators.

Antler Moth

The creamy-white, branching, antler-like mark gives this moth its name. Some examples are more convincingly antler shaped than this one.

RESULTS TABLES

Each column in the following two tables represents a week from early April to mid October 2018. The moth species which were trapped are listed on the left, and an X indicates the weeks when they were caught.[2] Sometimes more than one session was carried out in a particular week, and some weeks there was no trapping at all. 1437 moths of 142 species were identified over the 6 month

2 *In order to limit the size of the printed table, those species where 2 or less moths were caught have not been included. The complete table containing all sightings is available online at www.bailiesofbennachie.co.uk*

Table showing moths caught - total numbers and by week (excludes species with 2 or less captures)

	Total moths	APR 9th	16th	23rd	30th	MAY 7th	14th	21st	28th	JUNE 4th	11th	18th	25th	JULY 2nd	9th	16th	23rd	30th	AUG 6th	13th	20th	27th	SEPT 3rd	10th	17th	24th	OCT 1st	8th	15th
Yellow Horned	6	X	X																										
Chestnut	19	X	X	X	X																								X
Hebrew Character	204	X	X	X	X	X	X																						
Clouded Drab	83	X	X	X	X	X	X																						
Satellite	4	X	X																										
Common Quaker	97	X	X	X	X	X	X																						
Mottled Grey	12	X	X	X	X																								
Brindled Beauty	33		X	X	X																								
Twin-spotted Quaker	3		X																										
Early Tooth-striped	14		X	X	X																								
Engrailed	11		X	X	X				X																				X
Red-green carpet	9		X	X	X																								
Water Carpet	13		X	X	X		X	X	X	X	X																		
Brindled Pug	3		X	X	X																								
Scalloped Hazel	10						X	X	X	X	X																		
Nut-tree Tussock	30			X	X	X	X	X	X																				
Scarce Prominent	6					X																							
Glaucous Shears	35						X	X	X																				
Brimstone Moth	29							X	X	X																			
Brown Silver-line	6							X	X	X																			
Common Pug	5							X	X	X																			
Common Wave	3								X	X	X	X																	
Coxcomb Prominent	7								X	X	X	X																	
Flame Carpet	7							X	X	X										X	X								
Flame shoulder	3								X	X	X																		
Grey Pine Carpet	4								X	X	X																		
Knot Grass	3								X	X																			
Brocade	25							X	X	X	X	X										X							
Poplar Hawkmoth	14								X	X	X	X																	
Scalloped Hook-tip	4								X	X	X																		
White Ermine	6								X	X	X	X																	
Garden Carpet	7							X	X	X	X																		
Small Phoenix	7							X	X	X	X	X																	
Brown Rustic	7								X	X	X	X																	
Foxglove Pug	3								X	X	X																		

Table showing moths caught - total numbers and by week (excludes species with 2 or less captures)

Species	Total moths	APR 9th	16th	23th	30th	MAY 7th	14th	21st	28th	JUNE 4th	11th	18th	25th	JULY 2nd	9th	16th	23rd	30th	AUG 6th	13th	20th	27th	SEPT 3rd	10th	17th	24th	OCT 1st	8th	15th
Silver Y	60																												
Spectacle	3								x																				
Tawny-barred Angle	4							x	x																				
Silver-ground Carpet	5								x	x	x																		
Small Square-spot	22									x	x	x																	
Green Carpet	3															x				x									
Scalloped Oak	8																			x	x								
Mottled Beauty	10															x				x									
Smoky Wainscot	8															x													
True Lover's Knot	3															x													
Large Yellow Underwing	106															x	x	x	x	x	x	x	x						
Antler Moth	29															x	x	x	x	x	x	x	x						
Six Striped Rustic	12															x	x	x	x	x	x								
Riband Wave	4															x	x	x											
July Highflyer	56														x	x	x	x	x	x	x	x							
Ingrailed Clay	18															x	x	x	x	x	x	x							
Dotted Clay	37															x	x	x	x	x	x	x	x						
Small Rivulet	3														x	x													
Double Square-spot	3															x				x									
Common Carpet	3															x				x	x								
Common Rustic agg.	30																	x	x	x	x	x							
LBBYU	20																		x	x	x	x	x						
BBYU	3																			x	x								
Garden Carpet	7																			x	x	x	x						
Underwing	18																			x	x	x	x						
Rosy Rustic	29																					x	x	x					
Square-spot Rustic	47																		x	x	x	x	x	x	x	x			
Barred Chestnut	3																			x	x								
Brown-spot Pinion	12																							x	x	x	x		
Heath Rustic	6																					x	x						
Sallow	4																							x	x				
Pale Eggar																													
Red-line Quaker	3																											x	x
Autumnal Moth	4																											x	x
November Moth	3																											x	

LBBYU = Lesser Broad-bordered Yellow Underwing

BBYU = Broad-bordered Yellow Underwing

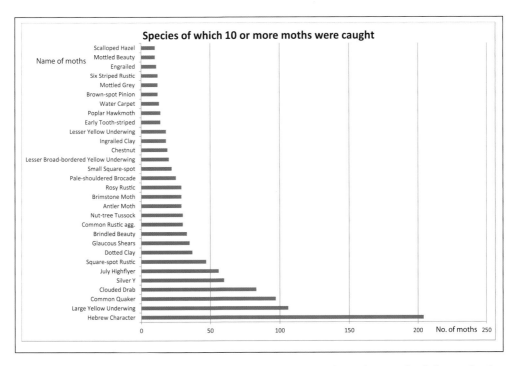

Species of which 10 or more moths were caught

survey. In 40 species only 1 individual was seen. At the other end of the scale the maximum trapped, over a period of 6 weeks, was a total of 204 of the species Hebrew Character. The chart shown above documents those species of which 10 or more moths were caught.

FLIGHT SEASONS

Individual moth species have a distinct flight season: the timing of which is important for particular parts of their life-cycle, typically associated with mating, egg laying, or availability of food plant. The diagram below illustrates the concept of flight seasons. The results shown in the tables above demonstrate that individual species were only trapped within the periods defined by their flight season.

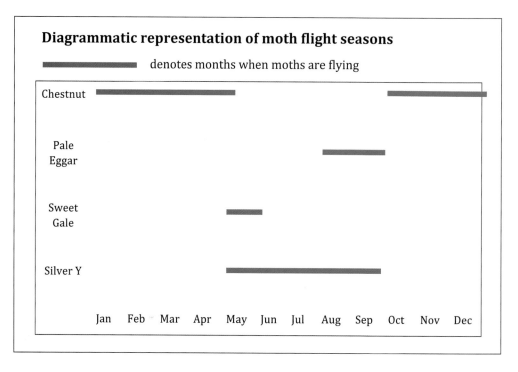

Diagrammatic representation of moth flight seasons

━━━━━━━━ denotes months when moths are flying

	Jan	Feb	Mar	Apr	May	Jun	Jul	Aug	Sep	Oct	Nov	Dec

Chestnut

Pale Eggar

Sweet Gale

Silver Y

Examples of Moth Lifecycles

The following are notes about those species which are highlighted in the results tables (above) in bold font. They illustrate how moths occupy particular niches in terms of habitat, food-plants and timing of lifecycle.

Yellow Horned

This moth does not have horns, but does have orange antennae from which it takes its name. It was caught in the first two weeks of surveying in early April. The adult moths emerge from the pupa in late February and are on the wing till mid-April. During this time they mate, lay eggs and then die. Its caterpillars then hatch from the egg around mid-May and feed voraciously until mid-July when they pupate among leaf litter on the ground. The pupa then passes the autumn and winter in relative safety until the adult moth emerges in early spring. This moth takes a full year to complete one cycle from egg to adult and many moths follow a similar pattern. Only a few species of moth over-winter as an adult. The majority survive the cold weather as an egg, a caterpillar or a pupa. Two species were identified which pass the winter as an adult – the Chestnut and the Red-green Carpet.

Chestnut

Chestnuts were trapped in April and again during October. This is typical for this moth which emerges from its pupa in late September and is active during the autumn. Over winter the adults are dormant in cold weather, but become active in mild spells, and in the Spring they mate and eggs are laid. The caterpillars feed on a wide range of broad leaved trees

Red-green Carpet

The Red-green Carpet has a slightly different strategy. When the adults emerge from the pupa in the autumn they mate, and the males having served their purpose then die. Only the females survive the winter to then lay their eggs in the spring, like the Chestnut, on various broadleaved trees of woodlands and hedges.

Pale Eggar

The Pale Eggar, which was trapped in August, is quite a widespread moth, particularly on moorland. It shows adaptations which allow it to cope at relatively high altitude. Typically the adults have a flight season from August to September. It survives the winter as an egg, hatching into a larva in April. In milder areas the caterpillars will pupate after about two months. However in upland areas, where growth is slower, it spends its second winter as a nearly fully grown larva, which then completes its growth and pupates in its second spring and summer thus taking two years to complete its life cycle.

Small Square-spot

The Small Square-spot was trapped in June, July, August and October. In the northeast of Scotland the eggs of this moth are generally laid around July. The caterpillars hatch a few weeks later and feed mainly on a range of herbaceous plants such as dandelion, docks and foxglove. This caterpillar typically eats at night and hides low down in the leaf litter by day. These plants keep a basal rosette of green leaves during the winter which allows the Small Square-spot to overwinter as a caterpillar, being dormant in cold spells, but becoming active and feeding in milder weather. In May the fully grown caterpillar pupates underground and emerges as an adult around June-July. In the south of England, where the climate is milder and winters shorter, the adult moths tend to emerge a month earlier, and it manages to fit in an extra complete cycle from egg to adult over the summer. It would seem that the good summer during 2018 allowed the Small Square-spots in this area to behave like those down south. The fact that they were caught over a five month span suggests that, unusually, there were two generations.

Silver Y

The Silver Y is a common and widespread moth which often flies by day, and can be seen nectaring at flowers along with butterflies. This moth does not survive over winter in Britain. In the spring these moths arrive in waves from southern Europe and North Africa, and spread throughout the country. They then lay their eggs on a wide range of both wild and cultivated herbaceous plants. There can then be two generations in subsequent months and these are supplemented by more migrants. In the autumn it is thought that the moths which grew up in the UK migrate south back to the countries from which their ancestors originated. 60 of these moths were trapped between June and August.

Left: Sweet Gale; Right: Glaucous Shears.

Sweet Gale and Glaucous Shears

The Sweet Gale Moth and the Glaucous Shears are both typically moorland moths and there have been very few records of the Sweet Gale in this area. Finding it was quite a significant result.

Slender Brindle

Some moths, which previously only occurred in the south of Britain, are extending their range and spreading north. The Slender Brindle used to be found only south of the border but since the 1980s it has spread north and is now resident in the southern half of Scotland and up the eastern side as far as Moray. The caterpillars of this moth feed on woodland grasses, at first feeding inside the stems and, later, on the leaves and flowers. They overwinter in the larval stage in tussocks of grass which remain green through the cold weather, give them protection and allow feeding in mild spells. When fully grown, the larva burrows into the soil, where it pupates in an underground cocoon. This is still a relatively rare moth in this area.

Pale Pinion

Even rarer is the Pale Pinion. Historically this was a moth of southern England, but, in recent years, presumably due to climate change, it has spread rapidly north and is widespread in the southern half of Scotland. It is only rarely recorded in NE Scotland. One individual was caught in April which would have emerged in the previous autumn and overwintered in some sheltered spot as an adult. In the spring they feed at willow catkins as a source of energy, then mate and lay eggs. The caterpillars feed on a wide range of broadleaved trees and shrubs.

CONCLUSION

Using a light trap regularly over a season opened a window into the world of moths. 142 of the 420 species which have been documented in NE Scotland were seen. Many of these were visually striking and showed remarkable camouflage and mimicry. Moths were found with different life patterns which have evolved to cope with seasonal change, particularly the challenge of surviving the winter. Bennachie supports moths from a range of habitats, and moths were caught whose larvae feed on grasses, herbaceous plants, shrubs and trees, and moorland plants. It was interesting to learn about the Silver Y moth which migrates here from the Mediterranean area. The unusually warm summer allowed the Small Square-spot to produce an extra generation, as typically happens in the south and, finally, the northward spread of the Pale Pinion is an example of the effect of climate change on moth distribution.

This initial look at the moth population has provided a base-line dataset upon which to build. Next season, it is intended to improve the design of the LED moth trap, in particular, by making it more easily transported by bike, and to carry out more frequent monitoring of moths at higher altitude on the Bennachie plateau. It will be interesting to observe the effects of varying altitudes and ecologies on the habits of the Bennachie moths.

If the reader would be interested in experiencing moth trapping, there are a number of public events during the summer organized by various agencies including the Aberdeenshire Council Ranger Service. The website of the East of Scotland branch of Butterfly Conservation lists all events and has helpful information on moth identification and listings of species likely to be seen in any given month. This can be found at https://butterfly-conservation.org/in-your-area/east-scotland-branch

ACKNOWLEDGEMENTS

Grateful thanks are due to a number of individuals, in particular, Helen Taylor for her hands-on help and support with the moth trapping and identification, and also for continuing with recordings when the author was on holiday. Helen Rowe, in her role as an Aberdeenshire Council Countryside Ranger, first introduced the author to moth trapping and, as Vice County Moth Recorder, provided great support and advice. Roy Leverton's patient explanations of the identification points of the various species, and expertise in acting as the final arbiter for moth identification, were invaluable. Margaret and Brian Garden generously provided the use of their garden (and electricity!) for mains trapping. Helen Taylor provided the photograph of the Small Square-spot; all others were taken by the author.

Druminnor Castle:
Report on the Geophysical Survey, 2019

Colin Shepherd and Emil Tanasie[1]

Introduction

As part of the ongoing excavations at Druminnor Castle - now in their eighth season - a programme of geophysical survey was undertaken in order to help understand the site better and to aid future excavation strategies. This work was generously sponsored by the Castle Studies Trust and undertaken by Alpha Geosurvey at the beginning of April, 2019. 2,500 square metres were surveyed using Ground Penetrating Radar (GPR) across a total length of five and a half kilometres. In all, 286 transects were recorded to a depth of just over four metres. 'Time slices', each of approximately 100mm depth, were compiled from these data to provide a view of the site through time. Two transects were also carried out using Electrical Resistivity Tomography (ERT). These were laid out on roughly north-south and east-west orientations and intersected between formerly excavated trenches. One ERT transect was 70 metres in length whilst the second was a little over 90 metres.

The Druminnor Castle excavations form part of the Bennachie Landscapes Project, run jointly by the Bailies of Bennachie - a local community-led conservation and research group - and the University of Aberdeen. Druminnor Castle is home to Alexander Forbes who is to be warmly thanked for all his help, support and important historical knowledge. All those working on the site are volunteers.

Historical Background

Druminnor Castle was the caput of the Lordship of Forbes. It sits within Kearn parish which, along with the parish of Forbes, formed the Barony of Forbes as recorded in a charter of 1271/2 (Ant. A&B, iv, 372) (Figure 1). Though the Forbeses are known to have been at Druminnor from this time, it is possible that they were associated with the site prior to this - the 1271/2 charter simply recording an earlier state of affairs. A grain-drying kiln, dated to the second half of the 12th century (Shepherd, 2018) indicates that the site was settled, probably in a 'manorial-like' fashion, at that earlier time.

---

1   Alpha Geosurvey, info@alpha-geosurvey.co.uk.

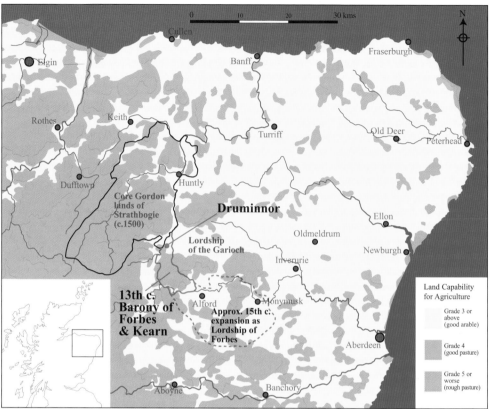

Figure 1. Lordship of Forbes and associated familial lands in the 13th and 15th centuries with land capability for agriculture (based upon Macaulay Institute, 1982).

Documentary study carried out for the Bailies of Bennachie in 2010 (Shepherd, 2011) revealed the hitherto overlooked survival of two 18th-century estate plans (RHP 260/1a; RHP 44705) detailing the plan of the castle (Figure 2). Prior to this, it had been considered that the castle had consisted simply of the present hall block with an attached tower on its north-west corner (Slade, 1967). This can now be shown to have been a completely erroneous view. Subsequent excavation as part of this project (Shepherd *et al*, 2015; in prep.) has demonstrated that the 18th-century plans are fairly accurate in their depiction of the castle with a main courtyard and appended, secondary court. The latter appears to have been added in the early 16th century, with the main courtyard being a product of the mid 15th century. A ditch-like feature underlying the buildings in the lower courtyard may well be related to the 1456 licence to fortify that notes permission *"to fortify the same with walls and circumvallate it with ditches..."* (Forbes, 2011, 1 ; Ant. A&B, iv, 400) (Figure 3). The upper courtyard appears to have been built upon a platform created by dumping a vast quantity of quarried sandstone to the

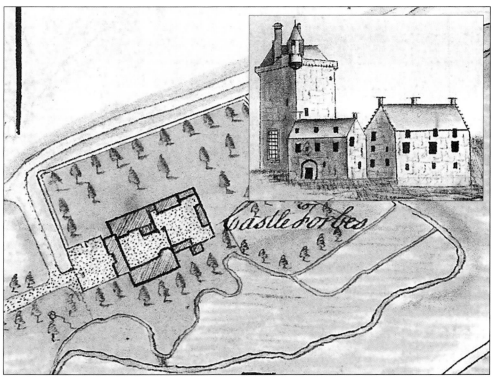

Figure 2. Two sections of one of the 18th c. estate plans (RHP 44705) showing castle plan and inset sketch of the standing buildings. Note the three courtyards and outer garden enclosure. Also, the interesting irrigation pattern below the castle.

height of a geological basalt dyke. This latter feature may have had a bearing on the siting of the castle. At least some of the platform material may have originated from the ditch beneath the later lower courtyard buildings.

Other features (apart from the kiln), lying to the north of the tower, have been revealed by the excavations and do not form part of the 18th-century plan. They appear to be earlier in date. These may relate to the 15th-century build or to a former plan associated with the tower, prior to the 15th-century work. During the 1600s, Druminnor was again refurbished, possibly resultant upon damage inflicted in 1571 by the neighbouring Gordons of Strathbogie, with whom the Forbeses were in an almost perpetual state of conflict. From the early 1700s, parts of Druminnor again lay in a state of disrepair as economic stress and other factors forced the then Lord Forbes and family to live elsewhere. The present hall block was probably tenanted and the other castle buildings are presumed to have fallen into decay (Wright, 2003, 28). Druminnor was sold to the Grant family who demolished the buildings and tower in 1800 (Leyden, 1903, 229). The hall block remained in residential use and, between 1841 and 1843, a Victorian 'mansion

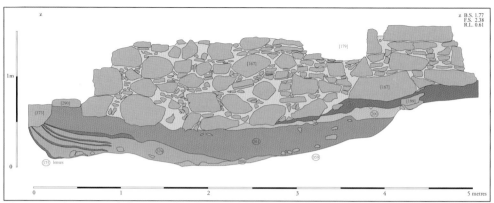

Figure 3. Section 94 showing later extended north barmkin wall with cut of ditch beneath.

house' was constructed against the north-west corner of the hall block. (This, along with other architectural evidence of a former adjoining structure, presumably led tŏ the supposition that the tower had formerly occupied that spot.) This 19th-century addition was itself removed in the 1960s.

AIMS OF THE GEOPHYSICAL SURVEY

The work reported upon here sought to address a range of concerns. Most were resultant upon previous excavation work that posed new questions and possibilites that, prior to those interventions, could not have been foreseen. Generally, these revolved around the fact that the site turned out to be far more complicated than first imagined. Another problem encountered was the intractable nature of the dense overburden of material comprising the present car parking area. In particular, help was required to help in deciding which parts of the car park showed the greatest archaeological potential. The tower is known to have stood on the site of the car park and former trial trenches had already demonstrated the difficulties involved in working in this location.

Previous work that revealed the kiln also raised the possibility that further remains may have been sealed beneath an area of lawn to the west of the castle. However, the overburden appeared to be almost two metres deep in places and a historically-important sycamore limits the potential for archaeological investigation in that area. Consequently, geophysical survey seemed to offer the only approach viable in such a sensitive area. This was also, as shown by the estate plans, the area of the 18th-century entrance to the castle and it was hoped that evidence may be found relating to that.

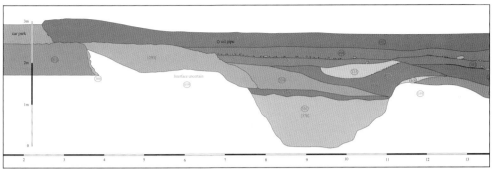

Figure 4. Part of Section 98 showing deeply cut feature of unknown origin partly overlain by platform comprising quarried and rammed sandstone.

Earlier excavations, as noted above, had also demonstrated the existence of a ditch-like feature that, it was hoped, might be traced by GPR as well as a much deeper cut feature (see Figure 4). The latter may be either archaeological or geological and the merits of both suggestions have resulted in hours of contentious wrangling between professional geologists involved with the project. (It was hoped that geophysics might sort the question before blows were dealt!)

Finally, the 18th-century plans depict an outer enclosure wall surrounding what may once have been formal gardens associated with the castle. It was hoped that GPR might pinpoint that feature in order that it might be sectioned.

Geophysical Survey Methodology

Ground Penetrating Radar (GPR)

The GPR technique uses high-frequency electromagnetic (EM) waves (from 10 to 3000 MHz) to acquire subsurface information (Figure 5). GPR detects sharp changes in dielectric uniformities in the different materials in the subsurface. These uniformities, in a geological setting, being a soil and rock material, water content, and bulk density. Data are normally acquired using antennas placed on the ground surface or in boreholes. The transmitting antenna radiates EM waves that propagate in the subsurface and reflect from boundaries at which there are EM property contrasts. The receiving GPR antenna records the reflected waves over a selectable time range. The depths to the reflecting interfaces are calculated from the arrival times in the GPR data if the EM waves propagation velocity in the subsurface can be estimated or measured. Equipment used was a Mala GX with 450MHz (approx. 150 - 900MHz) antenna.

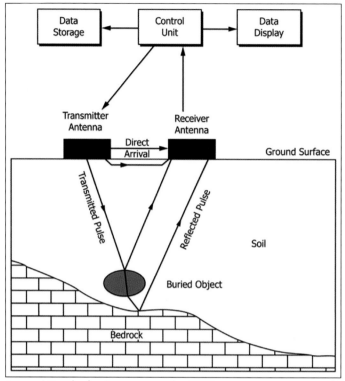

Electrical Resistivity Tomography (ERT)
(Also known as Electrical Resistivity Imaging - ERI)

Metal electrodes are used to inject an electric current and then measure that current. This determines the distribution of electrical resistivity in the ground and is closely linked to the nature of the ground material (Figure 6). Equipment used was an Ares utilising 48 electrodes.

Figure 5. The basic concept of a GPR system.

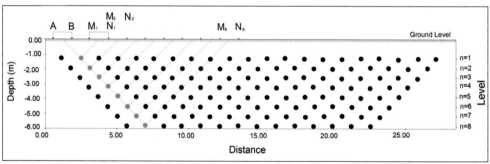

Figure 6. Typical data point distribution of an ERT profile using a Dipole-Dipole array.

GPR Data Coverage

The GPR data was acquired in grid patterns. In total there were 286 individual lines collected. The data was subsequently processed as a single data set to create time/depth amplitude slices - 'time-slices' (Figure 7).

Figure 7. GPR data coverage at Druminnor Castle.

ERT Data Coverage

The ERT data has been acquired as 2 intersecting profiles (Figure 7):

ERT1, 94m length, 48 electrodes at 2m spacing. Maximum estimated investigation depth: 18.8m

ERT2, 70.5m length, 48 electrodes at 1.5m spacing. Maximum estimated investigation depth: 14.1

Results and Archaeological Contextualisation of the Geophysical Survey

Of particular relevance for the present work at Druminnor are the results from the GPR survey. The 75 'time-slices' covering 2,500 square metres of the site of Druminnor have added greatly to its interpretation based upon known data as well as presenting foreknowledge for the planning of further interventions. These are now underway, informed by the GPR data.

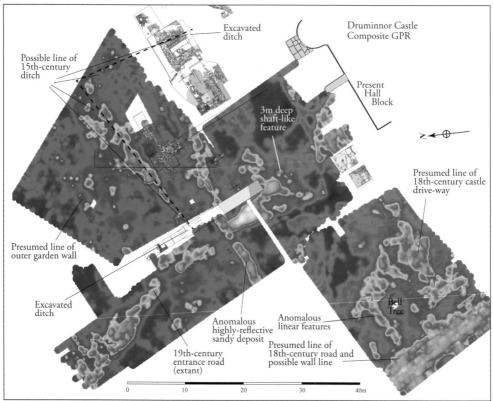

Figure 8. Composite view of all 0.5-1.8m time-slices showing major features.

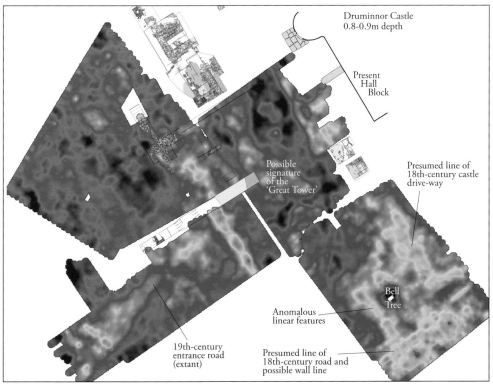

Figure 9. Reflective surfaces at estimated depth of between 0.8m and 0.9m.

Figure 8 shows a composite view of 0.5-1.8m time-slices, compressed onto a single dimension. In general terms, the red areas are the most highly reflective planes with respect to providing a contrasting interface between one surface and those above and below it. Three areas - the North Lawns, West Lawn and Car Park - have been indicated and will be referred to in the following assessment. Excavation trenches have been shown superimposed onto the GPR results.

Figure 9 shows reflective surfaces estimated to be between 0.8m and 0.9m in depth. In the North Lawns, the 19th-century entrance to the 'mansion' can be seen. This trackway still survives in a fairly grass-grown state. Its great depth, as shown by the GPR, is quite surprising but a consideration of the topography indicates that it was built up in order to maintain an even and level approach to the house. The natural ground level would have resulted in the road needing to dip before rising again to approach the house. Clearly, it was considered more appropriate to offer a level approach.

Within the Car Park area are a range of reflections that, it is hoped, indicate the presence of stone related to the tower. The difficulty of deciphering geology

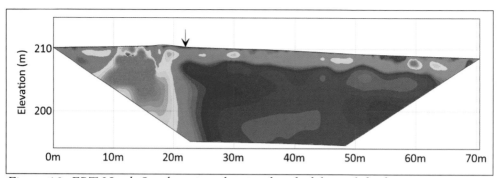

Figure 10. ERT North-South section showing basalt dyke on left of image.

from archaeology in this part of the site is hampered by the igneous intrusion that created the basalt geological dyke. This shows up as the large red expanse to the left on the ERT section shown in Figure 10.

The West Lawn shows a range of fascinating features. The linear features at the extreme west appear to relate to the known 18th-century entrance track to the castle. This appears to have been bounded to the east by a wall, as shown on the

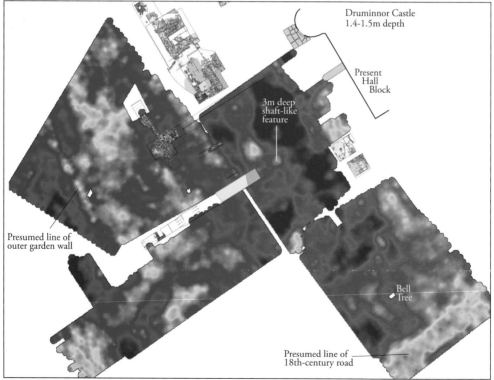

Figure 11. Reflective surfaces at estimated depth of between 1.4m and 1.5m.

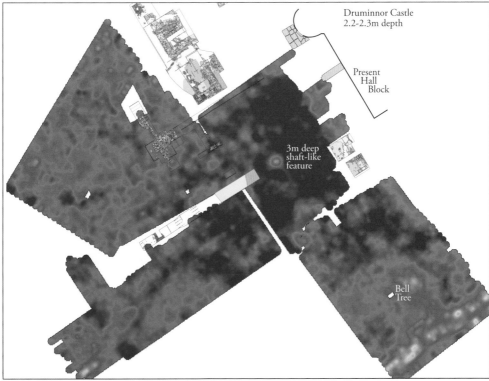

Figure 12. Reflective surfaces at estimated depth of between 2.2m and 2.3m.

GPR. There was a ninety degree turn into the castle approach and this also appears to be shown on the time-slices. These features appear to confirm the reasonable accuracy of the18th-century plans discussed above. Most intriguing, however, is the linear feature north of the Bell Tree. This may well be the northern boundary wall of the entrance court shown on the estate plan and might suggest that the Bell Tree was situated within this court.

The Bell Tree is an ancient sycamore and one of only a handful of 'named' trees recorded on the 1st edition Ordnance Survey maps. The reason for its name is lost to time, though a range of suggestions have been made. A late 19th-century photograph shows it looking fairly similar to how it does now and subsequent photos demonstrate that the present tree is, indeed, the same one photographed at that time. This would indicate that it was very old even then and it may be suggested that a 16th- or 17th-century planting date may be considered possible. The historical nature of this tree, therefore, militates against any archaeological work that would impinge upon its root system. Geophysical survey is, consequently, the only means available of assessing the below ground evidence here.

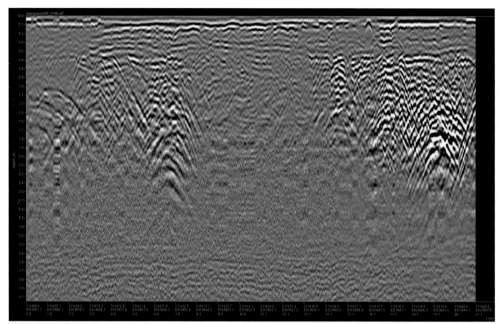

Figure 13. Radargram from transect 196 showing deep, circular shaft to the left of the central 'quiet' zone.

Figure 11 shows the time-slice at approximately 1.4-1.5m deep. The 18th-century entrance road is still clear and suggests that it was metalled to a substantial depth. In the North Lawns, a linear feature is likely to be the sought-after, northern enclosure wall as depicted on the 18th-century estate plan. Again, this demonstrates that the plan was fairly accurate in its depiction of the castle and its surroundings. In the Car Park is a circular feature within the footprint of the known location of the tower. Figure 12, at between 2.2 and 2.3m depth shows this feature continuing. In fact, it can still be seen at a depth of between 2.8 and 2.9m and seems to be about 2m in diameter. It appears to be a circular shaft filled with highly reflective material that extends downwards for almost 3 metres. It can be seen clearly on the radargram 196 (Figure 13) and it is hoped excavation will confirm what this interesting feature is. One obvious suggestion may be a well. However, its positioning in relation to the basalt dyke makes this an intriguing prospect and it may lay alongside the dyke within sandstone.

Finally, Figure 14 shows a time-slice at between 3.2 and 3.3m deep. Whilst most of the site is, at this depth, devoid of interest, the area around the Bell Tree still contains some highly reflective surfaces. In fact, this is the only part of the surveyed area that demonstrates features in all time-slices. It might also be noted that the present tree sits on a slight mound. Considering the depth of the 18th-century

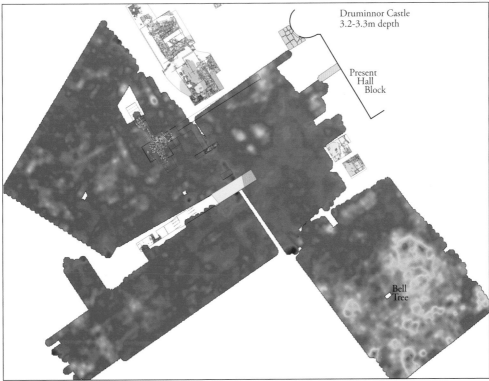

Figure 14. Reflective surfaces at estimated depth of between 3.2m and 3.3m.

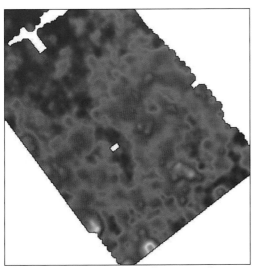

Figure 15. Area of the Bell Tree at the lowest time-slice of 4.1m.

road indicated by GPR, the tree must have loomed over the entrance track. Furthermore, if reflective surfaces survive at over 3 metres deep, it might be suggested that some stony structure may have been set upon the natural ground surface. This, presumably, has been subsequently added to by later deposits. Clearly, excavation is impossible because of the tree but the evidence to hand indicates that a historic, named tree sits in the middle of and above a pile of reflective deposits that are roughly circular and extend down for 3 metres. Even on the lowest time-slice at 4.1m, this feature is still evident (Figure 15).

CONCLUSION

Geophysical survey at Druminnor, as well as guiding future endeavours, has been used as a means of attempting to understand certain problems defined by excavation. This contrasts with how it is more commonly used when forming a predictive stage in site analysis, frequently culminating in excavation.

With respect to the aims of the geophysical survey, most have been achieved. The car park area has produced a range of disturbances that, it is hoped, relate to the former tower. Of particular interest is the deep, circular feature sited within the assumed footprint of that tower. Owing to the dense matrix forming the surface of the car park - accumulated over the last 150 years - this insight into the underground features is very important for increasing the viability of excavation in this area.

The West Lawn is virtually 'off-limits' with regard to excavation owing to the presence of the historically-important and aesthetically-beautiful ancient sycamore - the Bell Tree. GPR has been able to distinguish features recognisable from the 18th-century estate plan and to provide exact locations in order to plot these features accurately. Of particular interest has been the recognition that much of this ground has been substantially raised through time. The Bell Tree still sits on a slight, raised mound and when this is related to the 18th-century entrance track level as determined by GPR, can be seen to have towered over that feature. That further 'reflective' anomalies persist down to even lower depths raises the interesting possibility that this tree marks what was once a significant topographical, raised - possibly circular - feature.

On the North Lawns, the outer enclosure wall appears to have been recognised and can be targetted for excavation. It is hoped that dating evidence may be found in order to try to ascertain the date of this feature. More problematic has been the recognition of the ditches or 'cut' features recognised in previous excavation trenches. It is possible that the reflective anomalies seen on Figure 8 indicate stone 'backfill', thrown into the ditch after it had gone out of use. This theory will be tested by excavation. Finally, the very deep and equally puzzling cut feature shown in the section drawing (Figure 4) cannot be seen on the time-slices so far produced. It is presumed that the highly geologically-weathered sandstone is almost indistinguishable, in terms of reflective properties, from the fine sandstone-derived fill. Further analysis of the 2D radargrams is being pursued in the hope that more can eventually be gleaned from the data. It should be stressed that the analysis of the results is still ongoing. The data gathered in this survey can be sorted and ordered almost inifinitely to permit ever-closer refining of the results.

Figure 16. GPR survey on the West Lawn beneath the Bell Tree with surviving hall range in the background.

It is hoped that, in time, it will be possible to clarify the nature of that deeply-cut feature. But, with the exception of that outstanding 'work in progress', the geophysical analyses undertaken here have succeeded in achieving the aims set out and have provided important new data with which to develop further excavation strategies. Furthermore, a more accurate delineation of the castle plan has also been made possible by these results.

ACKNOWLEDGEMENTS

As noted at the beginning, this geophysical survey has been made possible through the generous funding provided by the Castle Studies Trust. As ever, grateful thanks are owing to Alex Forbes for his forbearance in the face of the ravages to his lawns and for his insightful historical advice. Bruce Mann of Aberdeenshire Council has, as ever, been a great source of support and advice as has Penny Dransart. Finally, were it not for the stout-hearted and highly-skilled volunteers of the Bennachie Landscapes Fieldwork Group who have been turning up for years to interrogate this site, its secrets would have remained hidden.

SOURCES

Illustrations of the Topography and Antiquities of the Shires of Aberdeen and Banff, Spalding Club, Aberdeen, Volume 4, 1847.

RHP 260/1a, Plan of that part of the lands of Forbes comprehending the parish of Kearn, c1771, National Records of Scotland.

RHP 44705, Plan of Braeside and Gartnach Hill, Aberdeenshire, 1770, National Records of Scotland.

BIBLIOGRAPHY

Forbes, A.   2011   Druminnor Castle, Documentary References and
                              Relevant Events, unpublished research.

Leyden, J.   1903.   Journal of a Tour in the Highlands and Western Islands
                              of Scotland in 1800, Edinburgh.

Macaulay   1982   Soil Survey of Scotland: Eastern Scotland, Aberdeen.
Institute

Shepherd, C.   2011   Landscape Changes around Benachie and the Garioch
                              during the Mediaeval and Post-mediaeval Periods,
                              c.1100 - 1800, unpublished, available at
                              www.bailiesofbennachie.co.uk

Shepherd, C.,   2015   *"Ecology and Landscape-use within the Pre-modern*
Irving, D.,   *Lordship of Forbes: Interim Report on Excavations at*
Groat, A., and   *Druminnor Castle, 2012 and 2013"*, in Shepherd, C.
Ralston, I.   (ed.), Bennachie and the Garioch: Society and Ecology
                              in the History of North-east Scotland, Bennachie
                              Landscapes Series: 3.

Shepherd, C.   2018   *"A 12th-Century 'bowl-fired' grain-drying kiln at Druminnor Castle, Aberdeenshire. Implications for Social Change, Agricultural Productivity and Landscape Development in North-east Scotland",* in <u>Studia Celtica</u>, 52, 1-32.

Slade, H.G.   1967   *"Druminnor, Formerly Castle Forbes: An Investigation into the Original Building of a Mid-Fifteenth-Century Palace House",* in <u>Proc. Soc. Ant. Scot.</u>, 99, 148-166.

Wright, A.   2003   <u>Druminnor Conservation Statement</u>, unpublished.

SHEPHERDS LODGE KAILYARD: PRE-PLANTING EXCAVATION

Barry Foster

INTRODUCTION

Shepherds Lodge is one of the colony houses on Bennachie. It formed part of the squatter settlement in the first half of the 19th century and was partially excavated in 2013 (Oliver *et al*, 2015; 2016). In 2017 members of the Bennachie Landscapes Project decided to recreate a kitchen garden or kailyard on the site of the original garden associated with the Shepherds Lodge house. In advance of this work, two small excavations were carried out in order to discover whether a garden footpath, as noted on the 1st edition OS map 1867 could be identified. This had

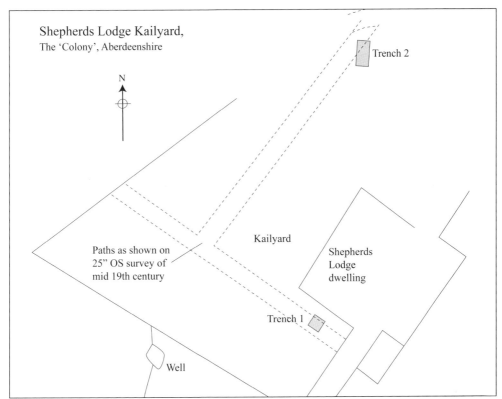

Figure 1. Measured survey of Shepherds Lodge kailyard with 19th-century paths taken from 25" OS plan placed in position.

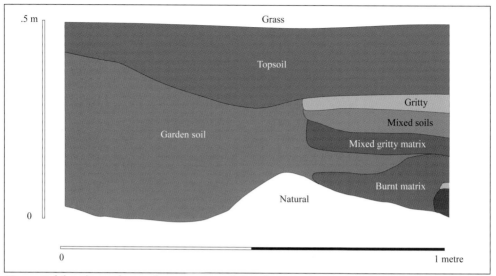

Figure 2 (above): south-east-facing section of Trench 1.
Figure 3 (below): south-west-facing section of Trench 1.

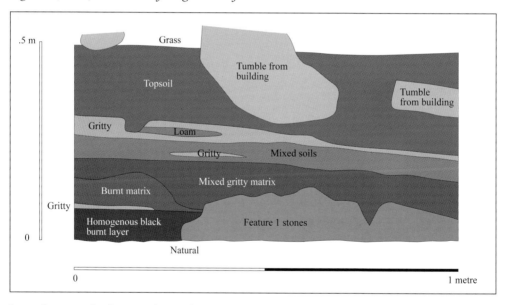

lain close to the house along the southern gable-end (see Figure 1) and a further path had continued across the kailyard to apparently exit on its northern-eastern edge. Trench 1 was opened in order to try to find the north-west to south-east path and Trench 2 was opened in order to look for the south-west to north-east path.

Trench 1

A 1x1 metre trench was opened and excavated down 0.5 metre until the natural subsoil was reached. No evidence was found for a built surface on the line depicted on the OS map, so it seems likely that the path shown there was no more than an earth-trodden path. However, on the east side of the trench nearest to the gable end of the house was evidence for a series of compacted surfaces that showed up well in section (see Figures 2 and 3 and Photo 1). These layers of gravels and mixed soils were sealed by a layer of topsoil that may represent 'soil creep' from higher up in the yard after the house was abandoned. (This was also evident whilst digging the garden plot for planting where a greater depth of topsoil was discovered at the bottom of the slope than at the top.)

The gritty matrices may represent a walkway around the house and appear to have accumulated over time. The homogenous burnt layer and the 'Feature 1 stones' may reflect initial site clearance and construction activity. It is noteworthy that a spread of garden soil overlays a deposit rich in burnt material (the 'Burnt matrix' in Figures 2 and 3) and may indicate an early depth of garden soil. This

Photo 1. Section of Trench 1 showing accumulated layers of gritty soils and underlying stone feature.

Photo 2. Shepherds Lodge with Trench 1 in the foreground and Trench 2 in the distance. The Littlejohns' house lies behind Trench 1.

was clearly increased over time. The remarkably large number of pottery fragments found in such a small area also suggests a thorough régime of manuring and soil improvement. This was also noted from other Colony sites (Oliver *et al*, 2016, 359). It might be assumed that the layers of deposits above this earlier spread of garden soil originally extended further from the house. But they all appear to have been subsequently cut back at the same time. Presumably, this was in order to extend and tidy up the garden edge later on in the site's history.

TRENCH 2

A 2x1 metre trench was opened to a depth of 0.5 metre down onto natural subsoil. This sought to establish whether the path depicted on the OS map did continue behind the house and whether it continued under the existing Forestry Commission path. Such a situation may have indicated that the property had extended further north. However, as with Trench 1, no evidence for a path was found. In fact, it appeared to contain nothing more than 0.5 metres of garden soil with 19th-century glass and pottery.

DISCUSSION

Shepherds Lodge was the home of the Littlejohns who lived on Bennachie from the 1830's until their eviction in 1878 (Fagen, 2011, 7). It is, therefore, quite likely that the house and garden were in use for over forty years. In that, quite short, period a house was built (and possibly extended), land cleared and cultivated, a home established, and a family raised. Garden plots would have been an important requisite to that lifestyle, supplying fresh food for the table: fruit and vegetables, a few chickens for eggs and meat, a milking cow for milk, butter and cheese and not forgetting the sheep of Shepherds Lodge!

Constantly-used paths around the house would need some sort of surface if they were not to become muddy channels for water to lay in. The fieldwork carried out at Hillside, another Colony house (Oliver *et al*, 2013; 2016), has demonstrated the care that could be lavished on such walkways and the work carried out in front of Shepherds Lodge (*ibid.* 2015, 89) may suggest a similar concern. Trench 1 considered here does suggest a metalled surface surrounding the house. This is where most frequent walking is likely to have occurred. But, what about the missing paths shown on the OS map? It might be suggested that they were little more than grassy 'baulks' left in order to access garden plots on either side. They would also have acted as a form of small-scale 'fallowing' - giving a patch of soil time to recover before the path was moved and a different strip left to run to grass for the season. It is hard to imagine that, were anything more permanent constructed, it could have evaded detection in both trenches and during the subsequent garden preparations.

SMALL FINDS

An impressive collection of 19th century pottery consisting of Rockingham ('Brown Betty') teapots, earthenware, brown and green bottle glass and clay pipe stems was recovered in the topsoil indicating the use of midden material on the garden.

ACKNOWLEDGEMENTS

I would like to thank Colin Shepherd, Colin Miller, Iain Ralston and David Peter for their help, both on the site, and later, and for their advice in the writing up of this summary of events.

BIBLIOGRAPHY

Fagen, J.   2011   The Bennachie Colony Project: Examining the Lives and Impact of the Bennachie Colonists. Bennachie Landscapes Series 1. Chapel of Garioch, The Bailies of Bennachie.

Oliver, J., Noble, G., Shepherd, C., Knecht, R., Milek, K. & Sveinbjarnarson, Ó.   2013   *"Historical Archaeology and the Bennachie 'Colony': Reflections on Fieldwork at a Nineteenth-century Site in Rural Scotland"*, in Shepherd, C (ed), Bennachie and the Garioch: Society and ecology in the History of North-east Scotland, Bennachie Landscapes Series: 2. Inverurie, The Bailies of Bennachie, 103-124.

Oliver, J.   2015   *"Archaeology and the Bennachie Colony: Excavations of Two 19th-century Crofts,"* in in Shepherd, C (ed), Bennachie and the Garioch: Society and ecology in the History of North-east Scotland, Bennachie Landscapes Series: 3. Inverurie, The Bailies of Bennachie, 83-98.

Oliver, J., Armstrong, J., Milek, K., Schofield, J. Edward, Gould, A. & Noble, G.   2016   *"The Bennachie Colony: A Nineteenth-Century Informal Community in Northeast Scotland"*, in International Journal of Historical Archaeology, 20, 2, 341-377.

The Bennachie Colony
Recreating a 19th-century 'Kailyard' (Kitchen Garden)

Christine Foster

Introduction

Aberdeenshire folk, native and new, are frequently intrigued by the 19th-century colony that once existed on the south-east slopes of Bennachie and much research has been devoted to this group of settlers. Unfortunately, very little was written by the colonists themselves so information about them is limited. What knowledge we do have is the result of countless hours of research by many individuals over a considerable number of years. Slowly this research is being pieced together and, although we are beginning to learn more, there are still many unanswered questions about their lives. One piece of evidence coming from the research is that each of the colony houses once had a 'kailyard' (kitchen garden) near to the house, independent of the small acreage of fields that were also part of the crofts. We have no definitive knowledge of what the colonists grew in these small plots or their methods, although we do know that the produce was for their own table and vital to their existence. So, what must it have been like for the colonists and what challenges did they face clearing and cultivating their plots - land that up until then had been deemed unfit for such purposes? What problems did they encounter, how successful were they as gardeners, what methods did they use, what did they grow, how did they source plants and what influence might they have left on the land? By attempting to answer some of these questions we hope to discover a little more about their lives and their effects upon Bennachie.

The Kailyard Project

Research in its different guises is ongoing and in 2017 a 'living history' project was undertaken to recreate one of the colony kailyards. By using methods and resources comparable to those most likely used by the colonists, we believed we might find answers to some of our questions. With joint funding from the Heritage Lottery Fund and the Bailies of Bennachie the project was able to go ahead. The timescale set was to have the plot suitably prepared and planted up by the end of the year. Thereafter it would be maintained by members of the Bennachie Landscapes Project who would keep a diary over the following few years and transcribe their findings. One of the objectives of the project was to encourage the local community to become involved by helping with its cultivation and monitoring the results.

The site chosen for the experiment was Shepherds Lodge, once the home of the Littlejohn family who built the house and worked the land there for over forty years. In 2013 the Bailies and the University of Aberdeen excavated Shepherds Lodge under a joint initiative. During this work scientific soil tests were taken and analysed by the University of Aberdeen, which gave an indication into some of the methods and skills of the colonists (Oliver *et al,* 2016).

No professional help was sought for the recreation of the kailyard, all volunteers were amateur gardeners or less, so most of our gardening knowledge has come from textbooks, past and present.

RESEARCH

Based on the assumption that the colonists would most likely follow similar methods to those of their forefathers, we focussed our research on agriculture in North-east Scotland during the 19th century. Consideration was also given to the effects of the agricultural 'improvements' that were causing major changes to the countryside at that time. When it came to decide what we might grow, there were certain limitations we had to consider in comparison to the colonists. Our main concerns were that there would be no one permanently on site to keep a constant watch on the progress of the kailyard or to tend the everyday needs of certain crops. The well at Shepherds Lodge, once used by the Littlejohns, dries up during the summer months and any water needed during the drier periods would have to be carried from the burns. Also, all tools and equipment would need to be carried up and down the hill for each work session. The decision, therefore, was to grow soft fruits, as they were perpetual and involved less intensive maintenance. Again, with our scant knowledge of what the colonists grew in their kailyards, research was based on local Aberdeenshire croft gardens during the 1800s with an emphasis on the type of fruit and varieties still in existence and available today. We opted for a selection of gooseberries, currants and raspberries and found a supplier that could cater for most of our needs, with a delivery date booked for early October.

FRUIT VARIETIES CHOSEN FOR THE KAILYARD

Blackcurrants:
Goliath* - Very old variety grown since before 1847.
Russian Black - Recorded in England in RHS records circa 1826.
Baldwin - A very old variety of unknown origin.

Whitecurrant:
White Versailles - Dates to the 1830's – recommended by Dr. Rex M Brennan, James Hutton Institute, Dundee.

Redcurrant:
Red Versailles - This is the red equivalent to the white, which was raised in 1835 – Recommended by Dr. Rex M Brennan, James Hutton Institute, Dundee.

Gooseberries:
Crown Bob*
Early Sulphur*
White Eagle*

Raspberries:
Gaia - Mixed old parentage including Black Raspberry* (pre 1860).
Heritage Raspberry

Rhubarb:
Prince Albert – Advertised in The Aberdeen Journal 1848.

* Indicates varieties listed in the 1860 Fruit Manual by Robert Hogg that quotes varieties of fruit being grown in Britain at that time (Hogg, 1884).

Unfortunately, the Early Sulphur and White Eagle Gooseberries failed. These were replaced with a Gooseberry cutting taken earlier from a bush found growing on one of the old colony sites (variety unknown) and a cutting taken from a modern variety ('Invicta' – claimed to be a very heavy cropper and mildew free). This will be used for comparative purposes.

With reference to our archival and soil research, we feel the approaches we have adopted are comparable to those of the colonists and have maintained an organic approach befitting the times.

Figure 1. Chosen kailyard plot after removal of broom and shrubs. (All photos by the author.)

INITIAL GROUNDWORK

Following a visit to Shepherds Lodge it was evident that our first on-site job would be clearing the overgrown broom, perhaps reminiscent of what the colonists themselves would have faced. Once the broom had been cut back and the whole kailyard area exposed, a plot of approx 25 square metres was marked out that would best suit our purposes (see Figure 1). We also carried out a botanical survey to check that no locally rare or interesting plants were evident. On the 1867 OS map Shepherds Lodge is clearly indicated showing the house and kailyard (see Figure 2). It also depicts a garden path within the kailyard, which was the subject of an investigation by the Bennachie Landscapes Fieldwork Group during 2017, when 2 exploratory trenches were dug. (See this publication: Foster, B., Shepherds Lodge Kailyard: Pre-Planting Excavation).

PREPARATION AND PLANTING

Over the next six months volunteers cleared the top layer of vegetation (mainly grass, weeds and old roots) and were pleasantly surprised by the good

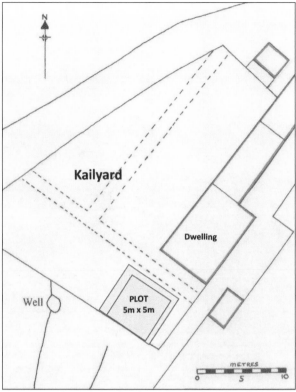

Figure 2. Plan of Shepherds Lodge kailyard and plot.

quality and depth of the soil (see Figure 3). Once the soil had been dug, weeded (and re-weeded several times!), we took a pH test, helped by the pupils from nearby Oyne School. In order to successfully grow soft fruit the results showed that we needed to reduce the acidity. We would also need to improve the soil using a suitable organic fertilizer. To help increase the alkalinity of the soil we used lime and, as fertilizer, locally-sourced horse manure. Another concern was the vulnerability of the plot from deer and (as suggested by the number of paw marks) dogs, so a fence was constructed around the plot. During the colonists' time the kailyard had a stone dyke built around its perimeter, evidence of which is still there today but, with our limited masonry skills, a cheap and easy alternative was to construct a fence. By using the timber and brash lying around in the nearby forest areas we felt we were within the cultural parameters of our objectives even though we were deviating from the known facts.

The kailyard was now ready for planting the heritage fruit bushes that we had scheduled for October. However, due to their late delivery we were not able to plant these until the last week in November, by which time winter had arrived bringing snow and ice (see Figure 4). This was followed by a hot, dry spring and early summer. Fortunately, the plants were of excellent quality and only two gooseberry and one raspberry failed. These were duly replaced, and a rhubarb crown also added, all of which were watered in using water carried up from the Clachie Burn as the well by this time had run dry. All the plants flourished and even gave a small crop of assorted fruits in the autumn (see Figure 5).

Figure 3. First dig after removal of all vegetation – note the good quality of the soil.

Figure 4. Working in the snow - planting and fence building.

Figure 5. Spring 2018 - Looking good, following a hard winter and dry spring.

OBJECTIVE

Our main objective over the years is to observe how the plants perform whilst being cultivated under similar conditions to those of the colonists. We have no knowledge of how successful the colonists were at producing their own food so can only surmise. But, we hope that by recreating this kailyard we will produce some evidence and new ideas concerning their probable challenges, triumphs and methods.

INITIAL OBSERVATIONS

The kailyard project has now been running for just over two years and throughout this time we have been recording our experiences and findings both through the research we have undertaken and from the hands-on work. Our final analysis will be completed at the end of the project but, in the meantime, the following are some thoughts, observations and suggestions for areas of further investigation.

Figure 6. Soil preparation - double digging and enriching the soil with horse manure.

While carrying out our research we were introduced to an autobiography by John Dickie of his early years in Aberdeenshire where he tells of his father who, in 1835, rented a piece of wasteland on the 'hill head of Balquhaine'. He quotes "The whins and broom at an average was from three to six feet in height and scarcely a foot of ground surface to be seen." He goes on to say that once these shrubs were cleared the stones were then collected for building a house. A plot of land was prepared and partially improved with lime yielding a crop "beyond the anticipation of all who saw it." (Harper, 2012)

When we first cleared the kailyard site of the overgrown broom, it was possible to visualise a little of what the colonists would probably have encountered, although we did not have the added difficulty of removing the stones and nor did our existence depend upon it! Following one day's work clearing the broom ourselves, provided a small window into the effort that must have gone into creating these crofts and a glimpse of the resilient characters who lived and worked there.

Results from the 2013 excavations and scientific soil tests at Shepherds Lodge provided evidence that the land had been well cultivated by the colonists. The tests showed a good depth of soil and areas of well drained land within the field systems. The kailyard provides further evidence of this via several factors.

Figure 7. A small selection of the pottery found in the kailyard plot.

Following the botanical survey, Creeping Soft Grass (*Holcus mollis*) was recorded 'fairly abundantly' in one area of the kailyard. Interestingly, this grass is found mostly on moist, freely-drained acid soils, normally light to medium texture and high in organic matter - a good indication that this soil had been well cultivated at one time.

Apart from trees, the plot had been lying dormant since the late 1800s and, once we had removed the broom and top layer of herbage from the plot, we were surprised to find such a large depth of good quality soil beneath, again proving that this land had been well worked by its owners in the past.

The considerable quantity of broken pottery and artefacts found while preparing this ground shows the colonists were improving their soil partly using domestic waste from their middens. The soil tests undertaken by Aberdeen University indicated that wood ash was present in the kailyard, possibly as a result of the contents from house fires being thrown into the midden. This would have helped decrease the acidity, but whether the colonists were aware of this fact is a question for debate. However, according to John Dickie his father was using lime on his fields in 1835, so it was something that the local farmers were aware of, and no doubt the colonists too. Despite being an impoverished farmer, Dickie Snr. still used lime which, presumably, he would have purchased. The colonists were in much the same situation, so the probability is that they too would have used lime on their fields. As the pH soil test we took showed a high acidity content, we decided to follow Dickie Senior's method and use lime as, apart from increasing the alkalinity of the soil, this also contains other valuable organic nutrients.

At the beginning of the project we studied old gardening techniques and compared them to modern day practices. We were surprised to discover how little difference there is in the recommended basic preparation of the soil today to those written by John Read in the 'Scots Gard'ner' first published in 1683 (Reid, 1988). His explanations of double digging and improving the soil (horse manure being one recommendation) are methods we still practise and ones we followed for the kailyard (see Figure 6).

As mentioned, a vast amount of broken pottery and artefacts were uncovered in the plot while we were preparing the soil (see Figure 7). This is providing a good insight into the type of crockery the inhabitants at Shepherds Lodge had been using and which are comparable to those already unearthed from the colony excavations of 2013 (see Taylor, 2015).

Another interesting observation came via the weather. The temperature often felt a degree or so warmer nearer to the house. This was particularly noticeable when we were planting the fruit bushes. It had snowed the day before and, although the sun was shining, there was a bitterly cold wind blowing across the hill that was very chilling. However, once closer to the house and kailyard the wind dropped due to the shelter of the higher land behind. The outlook from Shepherds Lodge has an exceptional vista too, suggesting this was no chance positioning for a home and must all be part of the equation as to why they chose to settle where they did.

The weather is a factor worth investigating further as there would have been good and bad years resulting in high and low harvest yields. How would the colonists have managed when harvest yields were low? Are there any significant events that are in the archives that could be linked to such times?

The question of herbs was raised on several occasions. There is no evidence of any having been grown but herbs are featured throughout history, as much or more for their medicinal uses than culinary, and the probability is that most households would have had a few herbal remedies to hand. These are all areas calling out for further research.

FUTURE

Over the next few years the kailyard will continue to be maintained and monitored and, hopefully, providing more information and a better understanding of the part it played in the colony's history. Meanwhile, a diary is being kept of all observations for analysis at the end of the project. This can be viewed on the Bailies' website. The kailyard can be viewed at any time.

ACKNOWLEDGEMENT

Grateful thanks to all the many volunteers who have helped over the course of the project, too numerous to mention individually, but includes the researchers, archaeologists, pot washers, gardeners, fence builders, carriers and carters, and those that are continuing to maintain a watchful eye over the kailyard. Special thanks to our young volunteers, in particular Jacob, for his boundless energy and enthusiasm, seen busily double digging and manuring the plot on a previous page. As the saying goes, "many hands make light work" and this has certainly been the case here. So, thanks to all who have played a part in this project and helped it along its way.

REFERENCES

Oliver, J., Armstrong, J., Milek, K., Schofield, J. Edward, Gould, A. & Noble, G.   2016   *"The Bennachie Colony: A Nineteenth-Century Informal Community in Northeast Scotland",* in <u>International Journal of Historical Archaeology</u>, 20, 2, 341-377.

Foster, B.   2019   *"Shepherds Lodge Kailyard: Pre-Planting Excavation",* in Shepherd, C. (ed), <u>Bennachie and the Garioch: Society and Ecology in the History of North-east Scotland, Bennachie Landscapes Series: 4, ..-..</u>

Hogg, R.   1884   <u>The Fruit Manual: a Guide to the Fruits and Fruit Trees of Great Britain</u>, London.

Harper, M.(ed.) 2013   Footloose in Farm Service: Autobiographical Recollections
                        of John Dickie, Aberdeen.

Reid, J.   1988   The Scots Gard'ner, Edinburgh.

Taylor, S.   2015   *"Pottery Finds from the Colony Site: Some Initial
                        Observations"*, in Shepherd, C. (ed), Bennachie and the
                        Garioch: Society and Ecology in the History of North-east
                        Scotland, Bennachie Landscapes Series: 3, 99-110.

Two Quarries on the Bennachie Colony

Andrew Wainwright

Introduction

There are two quarries on Bennachie within the area of the Bennachie Colony, which sits on the south-east corner of the Bennachie Massif. They are both situated in the woods close to Shepherds Lodge. The lower quarry is seventy-five meters to the west and the upper quarry is about one hundred meters to the north-west (see Figure 1).

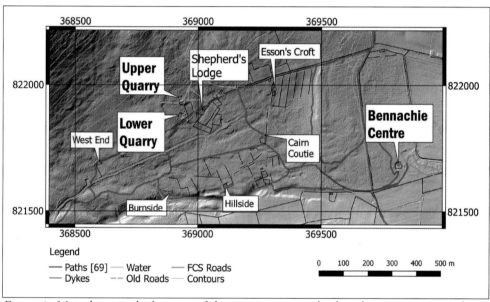

Figure 1. Map showing the location of the two quarries and colony houses superimposed on a LiDAR image.

The limits of the quarries are clear to see although they are somewhat overgrown. The lower one is right beside the path. The roads or tracks used to access the upper quarry and export the granite are also reasonably easy to find and they show up clearly on the LiDAR images.

The granite in both quarries is the normal Bennachie granite consisting of coarse-grained, pink feldspar and quartz. Biotite (a brown mica) is the main dark mineral although some of the quartz is also dark - similar to Cairngorm, but much too small to be of gem quality. The feldspar occurs also as isolated phenochrists

Photo 1. Back wall of lower quarry. Note horizontal and vertical joints. Also, the block in the foreground with drill and feather marks. (Photo by the author)

(extra-large crystals) up to about 50mm long. Joints (natural fractures) can be seen running both roughly horizontally and vertically through the rock outcrops (see Photo 1) and these would have facilitated the extraction of the material.

No tool marks have been seen on the worked faces of the quarry and so it is reasonable to suggest that the granite would have been extracted initially by using large wedges and big hammers. The wedges would have been forced into the natural joints until slabs broke off. The slabs would then have been moved to a work area where they could be cut into more marketable sizes. This may have been done with chisels and large hammers but, as a few blocks have been seen with signs of 'drill and feather' working, this method must also have been used for larger blocks (see Photos 1 and 2). The method involves drilling a row of slots about 2cms by 5cms and then hammering wedges in between two metal plates (the feathers). An experienced mason could tell just by the sound of the hammer on the wedges when the stone would split and he could also tell if the cut was going off the required line.

An earlier method of splitting blocks - also visible around Bennachie, was described by James Anderson (1794, 28-32) after visiting an Aberdeen quarry. He says they used a tool like a heavy hammer but with a blunt point on each end to cut slots a few inches long and much the same distance apart. Wedges were then banged into each slot, each one being hit in turn until the block split in half. He notes that it was possible to split blocks down to about 9 inches wide with this method and that the resulting blocks were quite suitable for general building work with no further finishing. For higher quality work the faces were dressed with a tool that sounds like a heavy adze and that then it would be difficult to get a knife blade in between two blocks. By the early 1800s the holes were drilled rather than cut with a pick (Anon., 1827) and blocks with signs that they were drilled can been seen in Photo 1. It appears that the difference may not be very useful for dating. The 'carved slot' method with rectangular or trapezoidal holes was clearly used before the end of the 18th century. Recent work in New England (Gage and Gage, n.d.)

report that the plug and feather method with drilled holes was used by farmers to split large field stones from 1823 but that the 'flat wedge' continued to be used alongside the drilled method.

The Upper and Lower Quarries

The lower quarry is shown on the first edition of the Ordnance Survey map of the area, which was surveyed between 1866 and 1867 and published in 1869 (see Figure 2). As the outline looks to be the same shape as it is today, the quarry was worked during the occupation of the Colony and not for long after the survey was made. Alexander Littlejohn lived at Shepherds Lodge during this period and we know

Photo 2. Modern example of 'drill and feather' method. (Photo courtesy of Anna Frodesiak)

from census records that he was a labourer in 1841, a stone dyker in 1851 and a mason after that (Fagen, 2011, 38). Therefore, it is possible that he extracted much of the granite from this quarry.

The upper quarry does not appear on the first edition map although the road up to it is shown to the east of the field lying east of the lower quarry. On the second edition, which was based on the same survey but revised in 1899, neither quarry nor the connecting roads are shown. Also, on this later map, all the land

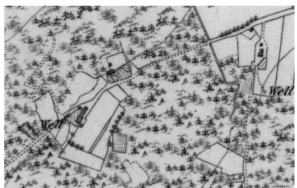

Figure 2. Extract from the First Edition Ordnance Survey, 1866-7.

at Shepherds Lodge is shown as covered in trees and the house is indicated to be a ruin. The only croft in the Colony shown on this map as being occupied is Esson's.

We have a copy of a tenancy agreement between the Tenantry of Balquhain (basically the laird) and James Esson dated 1870 (MS 2769/1/76/1). The lease refers

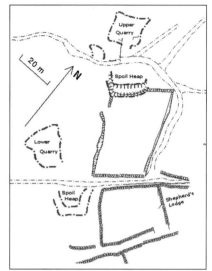

Figure 3. Sketch map of the two quarries and Shepherds Lodge.

to "the Quarry situated on the North side of Littlejohn's Croft". Two reasons make it probable that the quarry referred to here is the upper quarry. The spoil heap over-lies the top dyke of the Shepherds Lodge field to the east of the lower quarry and, of the two quarries, the upper one is the only one that could be described as north of the croft (though it is actually more NW). Since the quarry is not on the second edition map, work in it must have stopped before 1899 when the map was published. This quarry has not been surveyed in detail, but is a little bigger than the lower one. It may therefore have provided enough material for a similar number of dwellings.

No written record appears to survive to explain why the colonists opened these quarries. It might have been to provide stone to build their houses. Oliver (Oliver *et al*, 2016, 357) contrasts the houses on the colony with those in other informal communities in Highland areas where turf remained a common building material. He implies that the houses in the colony were stone-built because of the presence of the nearby quarries but then goes on to note that they were built of undressed granite. However, a cursory look around the area outside the cleared fields of the crofts would indicate that there was no shortage of suitable stones which could be dressed to some degree and used for building rough croft houses. The stones in the houses are of several different lithologies and often have rounded corners indicating that they were not quarried but are in fact field stones - or 'gatherings' as they are sometimes called. Also, the effort of quarrying the stone and transporting it to the further crofts in the Colony would have taken much more effort than gathering the stones they had to collect anyway, simply to clear their fields.

It is more likely that the stone was a cash crop for the colonists, or at least for Alexander Littlejohn and James Esson. Bennachie granite can be seen in all the farms and cottages around Bennachie that appear on the first edition of the Ordnance Survey map and it is also found in the older houses in Inverurie. Well-cut blocks were used for the lintels over windows and doors and for the corner stones. It was also used for the 'tabling' (the flat stones on top of the gable ends) and for 'spur' stones (those stones placed at the top of the corners of the walls to keep the tabling in place). On the cottages all other stones are field stones but, on more prestigious houses, the front wall was often built of quarried stone. Farm buildings were

Lower Quarry			
Isopach (m)	Area (sq m)	Vol. (cu m)	Tonnes
0	288.00	247.98	
1	210.00	165.67	
2	125.00	72.08	
3	30.00	10.00	
Granite Extracted.		495.73	
Lower Quarry Spoil Heap			
0	176.30	121.86	
1	74.60	38.08	
2	11.00	3.67	
Total Heap		163.61	
Void space	33.33	54.53	
Granite in Heap		109.08	
Granite exported		**386.65**	**145.91**

Figure 4. Volumetrics for lower quarry giving volume and weight of granite exported.

similarly built with field stones but with quarried stone for the important pieces. However, if a building contained a mill the walls would have used quarried stone; the rotation of a heavy mill wheel would have set up vibrations that would have been very destructive for a wall made of rounded field stones.

Buildings seen on the second edition map, but not on the first, are more likely to have been built using Kemnay granite. This granite has a white feldspar, the quartz is never smoky and the mica is white - not brown as in Bennachie granite. The Kemnay quarry opened for commercial operations in 1858. Although James Esson is quoted as saying that he thought Bennachie should be a major source of granite (Fagen, 2011, Figure 18), the fact that Kemnay was connected by railway, even though this was narrow gauge, made it that much more viable. Almost all the later buildings in Inverurie and many of the farms close to Bennachie are of Kemnay granite.

QUARRY SURVEY

The lower quarry was surveyed using taped offset and a dumpy level and a standard volumetric analysis was carried out (see Figures 3 and 4). This involved drawing contours on the bottom of the quarry, then extrapolating the contours for the surrounding ground surface over the top. The former was then subtracted from the latter and isopachites (contours of equal thickness) drawn for the thickness of granite removed. From this data, the volume was calculated by making the assumption that the volume between two adjacent isopachites was represented by the product of the interval and average area. (Alternatively, the volume could be calculated from the area under the graph of area against height.) Since the granite was dressed at the quarry and the waste dumped in the spoil heap, in order to estimate the volume of rock actually exported, the amount in the spoil heap had to be subtracted from the volume dug out of the quarry. The rock fragments in the spoil heap were simply thrown in and so large voids existed and these had to be estimated. Without doing detailed experiments and measurements, it was considered reasonable to use a figure of one third for this. Finally, the volume extracted was converted to weight by assuming the density of granite to have a specific gravity of between 2.6 and 2.7 (edumine.com).

In order to gain an idea of the use to which the quarried granite may have been put, two local houses were studied in some detail. Both may be considered typical of houses in the area as shown on the first

Photo 3. Burnside of Braco. Small four roomed cottage. Note the stones on the gable end, all with rounded corners. These are field stones that have been dressed to some degree. (Photo by the author)

edition Ordnance Survey map. The first was Burnside of Braco: a small cottage originally consisting of two rooms downstairs and two small bedrooms above. The measurements of the principle stones were taken for a sample of the main features. Thus, lintels and sills were measured as were the corner stones down one side of the door and one window. The other sides were assumed to be the same. The same technique was used on other features. The faces of some stones could not be seen because of being covered by plaster or framing and these had to be estimated. Similarly, some features such as the chimneys, could not be examined close up and so, here again, the measurements were estimated. Using this method, it can be suggested that the total volume of quarried granite used to build this one cottage was approximately 4.9 cubic metres.

Photo 4. Broadsea. This is a much larger house than Burnside of Braco. Note the blocks on the front are all well-dressed, quarried stones whilst those on the gable end are field stones. (Photo by the author)

The second house considered was Broadsea. This is a farm house and would have been considered of much higher status. There are also farm buildings to the side of it. Befitting its status, the front face comprises standardised blocks of the same rock type and colour. They are all clearly from the same quarry. The same estimations were used as on Burnside of Braco and, where the stones could not be reached, sizes were estimated entirely by eye. Because of its larger size and the nature of the front face, the quantity of quarried granite was estimated to be about 24 cubic metres - five times as much as was used in the cottage. The amount of quarried granite in the farm buildings is difficult to assess as they have been modified over the years and it is hard to see what is original. However, the amount of quarried granite in the south-westerly wing, which is where the mill was located, amounts to at least 18 cubic metres. There is also a small cottage behind the farmhouse.

So, the total amount of quarried granite used in the Broadsea farm might be estimated as 24 cubic metres for the house, 5 cubic metres for the cottage, 18 cubic metres for the mill and an estimated further 5 cubic metres for other farm buildings; a total of 52 cubic metres. Our quarry could, therefore, have produced sufficient granite to build seven or eight similar farms.

Conclusion

These two houses are typical of the domestic buildings found in the area. Although smaller cottages without any upstairs rooms do exist, farmhouses significantly larger than Broadsea, have not been noted. Many of the farms had bothies and small houses nearby for farm servants and the farm buildings were variable in layout and size. The first edition of the Ordnance Survey shows about forty farms and cottages in the immediate vicinity of the colony quarries - within a radius of about four kilometers. Most of these have not been studied and so their size and the sizes of any associated buildings have not been counted. Also, in the area, there are two bridges in Burnhervie and a church in Chapel of Garioch, all of which are shown on the same first edition map but could have been built before the quarries opened. Many of the older houses in Inverurie are also built using Bennachie granite. As there are no quarries for this material closer than Bennachie, this may well have been the source for all of these buildings. From the figures given above, the quarries in the colony would have been too small to provide all the granite for all of these buildings. Other quarries do exist on Bennachie and Millstone Hill but details of size have not been recorded. Presumably they were sufficient to provide the shortfall.

ACKNOWLEDGEMENTS

Thanks are due to Rosemary Webster who helped in the survey of the Lower Quarry and to Graham and Elizabeth Harper, and Laura and Michael McGhie who gave permission to use information about their houses for this paper.

SOURCES

MS 2769/1/76/1, Bundle of expired leases, Special Collections, University of Aberdeen.

www.edumine.com/xtoolkit/tables/sgtables.htm

REFERENCES

Anderson, J.   1794   General View of the Agriculture and Rural Economy
                        of the County of Aberdeen, Edinburgh.

Anon.   1827   The Builder, 35, 181 October 14.

Fagen, J.   2011   The Bennachie Colony Project: Examining the Lives
                        and Impact of the Bennachie Colonists, Bennachie
                        Landscapes Series: 1

Gage, M. &   n.d.   StoneStructures.org
Gage, J.

Oliver, J.,   2016   "The Bennachie Colony: a Nineteenth-Century Informal
Armstrong, J.,   Community in Northeast Scotland", in International
Milek, K.,   Journal of Historical Archaeology, 20, 2, 341-377.
Edward Schofield, J.,
Vergunst, J., Brochard,
T., Gould, A. & Noble G.

A Study of the Historic Carvings on the Mither Tap, Bennachie

Moira Blackmore

Introduction

This paper will consider some of the names and dates that have been carved into the granite outcrop at the top of the Mither Tap, Bennachie in North East Scotland. This topic stems from research undertaken for a dissertation leading to an undergraduate Archaeology degree with the Department of Archaeology at the University of Aberdeen. The carvings are an interesting and understudied part of the archaeology of Bennachie. This study addressed the practicalities of some methods for recording the carvings and attempts to make some suggestions regarding the identities of those responsible for those marks. A second topographical focus for this research was the nearby summit of Oxen Craig.

Bennachie has been an important feature of the landscape for thousands of years as evidenced by the many associated archaeological remains. Since at least the 19th Century it has also become a visitor 'hotspot', attracting walkers, hikers and local families. It gives the best views of the lower part of Garioch towards Oldmeldrum and Inverurie in the east (McConnochie, 1890). The landscape that surrounds Bennachie has a compelling and textured history and people have made their mark on the Mither Tap in many ways. The Mither Tap is the distinguishing feature of Bennachie, albeit not the highest point (that is taken by Oxen Craig) and the top of the Mither Tap is encircled by a Pictish fort.

Background

People have been leaving graffiti and other marks on the landscape for centuries. By looking at other types of graffiti around the world this may offer us a glimpse into who may have been climbing the Mither Tap at this time. Graffiti has for long been recognised as a means of interpreting the social, political and domestic life of the ancient world (Frederick and Clarke, 2014). Graffiti has been found at Pompeii and it relates to political statements and leisure activities. The Romans also used graffiti to put across political statements and used graffiti as a voice of protest (Keegan, 2006). Vikings left runic graffiti inside Maeshowe in Orkney when they broke into the tomb. These consisted of their names and information about other peoples and some of their values; they also left a drawing of a dragon (Historic Scotland, 2015). This type of graffiti gives us a snapshot of the past with historical and social details of the time. Graffiti can provide historians and archaeologists with an intimate and subjective view of society from a specific time. It offers us a window into their world and the minds of those who created it (Champion, 2015).

Most of the carvings on Bennachie are found on Mither Tap, where there is a commanding view over the extensive surrounding landscape. It was a place people wanted to visit and people maybe had lunch up there while they were working on the hill. Climbing the hill may have given a sense of achievement for some. The Mither Tap was part of the everyday lives of the people who lived in the Garioch. Not only was it a prominent feature of their landscape but it also impinged upon their world view. In the 19th century the working week was changing and there was more leisure time for some (Oliver and Neal, 2010). Local people were clearly going about the hill before the 19th century but we have more limited historical evidence of this. From the 19th century onwards there was an interest in the area from landowners, academics and other people using the hill for its resources. There were many estates in the area and the local gentry will have been showing their visitors around their landscapes. There were also farm labourers who would have traversed the area as well and, perhaps in their spare time, they climbed the hill, or had to climb it as part of their work. At the start of the 19th Century there were several industries at the foot of Bennachie. These included quarries, a sawmill and wood cutting (Watson, 1999). There were several major quarries and many smaller ones on Bennachie. Lintel Quarry, Little Oxen Craig and the English quarry show the most evidence of quarrying activity.

Early in the 19th Century, families moved to the hill of Bennachie - some from neighbouring villages. This was when the Bennachie Colony started, and it continued to grow throughout the 1840s and 1850s (Fagen, 2011). By 1851 there were about 56 people living on the hillside. The Bennachie Colony was a crofting settlement on the slopes of the Mither Tap at the east end of Bennachie. This was made up of some from the poorest class. People with no home used the materials found on the hill to build houses for their own occupation (McConnochie, 1890). The Colony was similar to a settler community as they lived by crafting and supplemented their income by working casually at quarrying, stone masonry, stocking-knitting, domestic service and drystone dyking.

The railway eventually became important for connecting Bennachie with the wider world. In the mid 19th Century there were several ways to get to

Bennachie and the advent of the railways increased access. They offered the public a more affordable transportation to the Garioch area and helped to stimulate a new interest in tourism. Connected to Aberdeen Joint Station were four stations that served Bennachie: Pitcaple, Oyne, Kemnay and Monymusk. One of the best-known routes was to disembark at Oyne station and ascend from the Back O'Bennachie (*ibid.*).

Alex. Inkson McConnochie was an avid climber and one of the founders of the Cairngorm Mountaineering Club. This group was making regular excursions to the hills of Bennachie between 1893 and 1930. The trips normally occurred during the summer and autumn months and were detailed in the local newspapers of Aberdeen. From what is documented in the local newspaper, we know that people were picnicking at Bennachie from the late 19th Century onwards. Visitors included local people from Aberdeen as well as members of athletic and mountaineering clubs that had annual trips out to the country. They would take the new railway out to one of the stations close to Bennachie and then proceed to climb the Mither Tap.

> *"Bennachie has its moods, so to speak; for in a bright, clear day the naked eye can detect miles away the paths and gordes running down the side of the hill; and again, there are times when Bennachie is dark and frowning, which may mean in certain seasons bad weather, or in winter a fresh setting in after the frost." (Beaton, 1915, 1)*

Methods for Capturing the Carvings

An important part of this research was to establish an efficient method for recording the carvings. Methods tried included: photography, sketching, sand, water and tracing. Some of these methods worked well and some did not work at all. The way rock art has been recorded in the past has provided a guide to recording these carvings. These methods seek to minimise damage to the art and to the rock surface itself (Sanz, 2014). The table below outlines the methods tried in order to capture the carvings on the Mither Tap.

Photography

The carvings were photographed individually using a digital camera with: a small scale; a one meter scale; and without a scale. They were captured in 'raw' format by the camera and were then converted to 'jpegs'. The carvings were best

Method	Materials	Did it work	Notes
Photography	A digital camera	Yes, it worked	This method was best done on a cloudy day as there was a problem when it was sunny as shadows got into the photographs
Sand	Coloured sand	Yes, it worked but it was messy	The sand sort of helped to bring out the carvings but it was messy and trying to keep it contained in the carvings was problematic.
Water	A spray bottle	Yes, and was best when it was sunny	Spraying water on the carvings helped but the water could not be controlled through the spray bottle.
Sketching	Waterproof graph paper and a planning frame	Yes, it worked	This method was used to pick up any detail the camera may have missed. Limited equipment can be taken up the hill.
Tracing	Tracing paper and charcoal	No	The ground was too rough and uneven for this method to work. It works best on a smooth surface.

Figure 1. Table of list of methods that were used to capture the carvings.

captured on a cloudy day as, when it was sunny, there was a problem with shadows hiding detail.

Sketching

Sketching is considered to be one of the most effective methods to gain an overview of a site that can lead to a clearer understanding and interpretation of that site (RCAHMS, 2011). The carvings on the Mither Tap were recorded using a standard one meter by one meter drawing frame and sketched onto waterproof graph paper. The sketch was labelled using a compass to record the north point, along with the name of the site and the date. Capturing the carvings in this way meant that the eye could sometimes pick up more detail than the camera lens.

Tracing

Tracings were also attempted in order to capture the carvings. However, this method was found to be a less successful method as the granite was far too rough and uneven. This approach was tried in order to investigate whether it might complement sketching as a way of capturing detail that may have been missed by sketching.

Figure 2. The Mither Tap, Bennachie covered in mist. (Photo by the author)

As can be seen by Photos 2 and 3, weather can play an important part in recording an open-air site like the Mither Tap where there is little shelter. Winds are stronger on the hill than at ground level and make recording difficult. Wind-free conditions with a lightly-overcast sky make for good recording weather.

Figure 3. The Mither Tap on a good day. (Photo by the author)

The Carvings

The top of the Mither Tap is a rocky granite tor of a reddish, binary compound of quartz and felspar culminating in a flat-topped area about 16 metres long. It is bumpy, uneven and 518 meters in height (McConnochie, 1890). The carvings are scattered across the top of the Mither Tap. They are not carved deeply into the granite, probably because it is such a hard rock to carve and they measure from 30cms to just over a metre across. The siting of the majority of the carvings gives the visitor a good view of the surrounding landscape. Not all the carvings are easy to access, with some located down in a gully and difficult to get to.

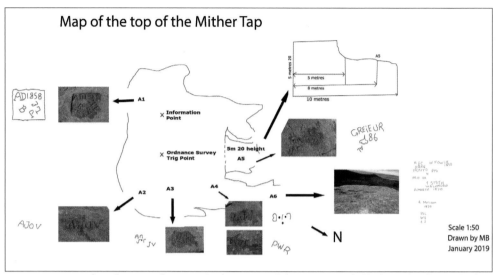

Figure 4. Map of Mither Tap showing the locations of the carvings. (All photos by the author)

Well-known carvings include the marks of the Commonty (known locally as the 'thieves' marks'). Carved as a square into the granite bedrock are the letters 'B', 'P', 'LE', and dated 1858 (Figure 5). The letters represent the initials respectively of Balquhain, Pitcaple and Logie Elphinstone. These indicate the local estates that meet at the summit of the Mither Tap and record the division of the Commonty in 1859. Alison Kennedy's work, looking closely at the census records, parish records and statutory records have given us suggestions regarding who may have carved some of the other marks (Kennedy, 2019). The following are just some of the carvings that have been identified by Kennedy, but many others are still shrouded in mystery.

'AL' may suggest that Alexander Littlejohn (either senior or junior) carved his initials into the granite tor (see Figure 6). The Littlejohns were the first documented family to break ground within the colony, relocating from the Balquhain estate sometime between 1834 and 1838. Alexander was one of the original colonists and was renowned as a mason and drystane dyker. He would certainly have had the tools to carve his initials into the granite tor.

In Figure 6, it is possible to make out a tree-like carving. Could this be a mason's mark for someone who had worked in one of the Bennachie quarries or as a stone mason? This seems an unusual image to carve and it is not like the majority of the carvings. Often, it has been suggested, mason's marks were made on stones during the construction process as a way of demonstrating which stones had been prepared by themselves - thereby keeping a tally of the payment required. Their

Figure 5. The mark of the Commonty - one of the 'Thieves' marks. (Photo by the author)

unique signature would associate only them with that piece of work.

'W Fowlie 1850' (Figure 7). There were two 'William Fowlies' - possibly father and son - living at Monymusk. The elder one was a 'saw-miller', and the younger a 'horseman'. However, there were 18 males indexed with the name William Fowlie, aged between 14 and 80, living in Aberdeenshire and noted in the 1851 Census.

'D Rae' (Figure 7). There were three 'D. Raes' on each of the 1841 and 1851 censuses for Aberdeenshire and all named David. In 1841 there was a David Rae, Cattle Dealer, living at Thainstone, Kintore, who may have been one of the 'artists'. In 1851, two lived in Pitsligo and one lived in Old Machar, Aberdeen. The one in Old Machar was a Quarrier, aged 28. Another D. Rae was found later in the 19th century in Aberdeen who was also a stone mason. There is no obvious date for this inscription and it could have been inscribed at any time by any of the above.

'T Smith' (Figure 7) might be a Thomas Smith and there were 36 men with that name on the 1841 census and 34 on the 1851 census all aged between 14 to 80 and all living in Aberdeenshire. Locally, there were a couple of Smith families living in Chapel of Garioch in 1840s and one of them may have made this mark.

Figure 6. Carvings in section A5 down in the gully with water sprayed on it to bring out the carvings better (Photo by the author)

Figure 7. Overview of the carvings in section A6. (Photo by the author)

'A Martin 1820' (Figure 7) may be Alexander Martin, although there was also an Andrew Martin shown on 1841 census as living in Aberdeenshire. The 1841 census lists 8 possible male carvers, aged 30-80 (based upon an assumption that, at the time of carving, the person had to be at least aged 10) living in Aberdeenshire. The 1851 census (aged 40-90) lists 9 possibilities. There was a shoemaker with an appropriate name living in the parish of Premnay and born in Oyne who was listed on both censuses. Whilst on the 1851 census there was an Alexander Martin, aged 80, living with his wife and sister-in-law, at Hill of Fetternear. All were listed as paupers, though Alexander was formerly a farmer.

'R Murison 1820' (Figure 7). R. Murison and A. Martin may have been inscribed at the same time if dates are correct. In 1841 only one R. Murison appears for the whole of Scotland and shown as living in New Pitsligo, aged 74 and his occupation was noted as a stone mason. He does not appear on 1851 census and had probably died in the interim period.

'W S' (Figure 8) could be William Selbie (Selby) born in 1802 in the Chapel of Garioch and who lived locally at Cumingstone (various spellings). William lived with his mother, Ann Cumming, although there are some references that he may have lived on Bennachie, possibly on a temporary basis. William was a mason and stone dyker and died in 1873.

Figure 8. Carvings in section A4. (Photo by the author)

CARVINGS ON OXEN CRAIG

There are also carvings on Oxen Craig and one of the most prominent carvings is 'R Queen, 1945' (Figure 9). This may have been made by almost anyone at this date. It may even have been someone living outwith the area who left no other record of his visit, apart from the carving. Maybe it was an overzealous new father, grandfather, or other relative, carving out a newborn's name on top of Bennachie! The carvings might not always be name of the inscriber. Perhaps this person had seen the carvings on the Mither Tap and thought it would be appropriate to carve their name on Oxen Craig.

Figure 9. Carving on Oxen Craig. (Photo by the author)

Figure 10. Carving on Oxen Craig. (Photo by the author)

INTERPRETATION

Some of the carvings have dates alongside the names which we can place in the 19th Century. Why did people carve their names into the top of the Mither Tap? Would the artists have been known locally or would they be anonymous? Were they intended for others to see or were they more private gestures? The carvings are somehow intimate but not hard to find or anonymous.

Alex. Inkson McConnochie's Book 'Bennachie' wrote that he noticed people had left their mark on the Mither Tap:

> *"The rock on top is disfigured by visitors who have left their 'mark' behind cut out on the rock." (McConnochie, 1890, 48-49)*

McConnochie treats the carvings as mindless vandalism, linking them to the desecration of nature. We need to ask however, whether others shared that same perspective. People in the local area may not have seen the carvings as mindless vandalism and, perhaps, saw it as making a mark on the local environment. It might, therefore, be interpreted as a claim to 'ownership' of the landscape.

Granite is recognised as a difficult material to work and an accomplished craftsman might be considered necessary to achieve these results (Donnelly, 1975). Most of the names and initials are very skilfully incised and they do not, necessarily, seem to be what all might call vandalism. If some of the people who visited the hill were masons, quarry workers and drystane dykers, this may be a reason why they are so well-carved.

The stone masons and the men working in the local quarries would, presumably, have had tools to carve the rock at their disposal and may have taken them along when they climbed Mither Tap. These tools might have included a hammer and chisel. To work the stone they would have required a steady eye and a sureness of touch (*ibid.*). Some visitors to the hill may not readily have had tools at hand and they may have used something like a pocket pen knife, though how that would have fared against the granite, perhaps, requires some experimental work.

Conclusion

Have the carvings changed the way that people look at the Mither Tap in the landscape and do they make people think about the hill differently? It is not just a hill to be climbed and celebrated when you make it to the top. The hill is not just about the Pictish fort that crowns the top of the Mither Tap. It is about the carvings at the top of the hill as well. Many people simply look at the view when they get to the top - which is quite understandable as the Mither Tap gives a 360-degree view of the Garioch countryside.

By attempting to understand who was going about the area at the time of the carvings may give some clues as to the types of people who may have made the carvings on the Mither Tap and Oxen Craig. We know people were living on the hill in the Colony, landowners were shaping the countryside and the advent of the railway was bringing people out into the countryside. By considering how other rock art was recorded has helped in developing a method to record these carvings. With the help of Alison Kennedy it has been possible to suggest some possible histories to some of the names carved, but others remain shrouded in mystery.

Many people clamber up the Mither Tap, especially at weekends, and it is becoming an increasingly popular venue. The pathways to the Mither Tap are kept clean and well preserved by the Bailies of Bennachie, helping to aid access. Increasingly, the carvings are under threat of being worn away, not just by the visitors, but also by the weather. Posters and leaflets have been created for the Bennachie Centre to display during the summer months in order to encourage visitors to think differently about the hill and to consider the fact that history even survives below their feet as they walk across the top of the Mither Tap.

Future work aimed at recording and anlaysing the graffiti might take the form of photogrammetry. This photographic method records a three dimensional image of the carvings (Sanz *et al*, 2013) and may mitigate, in one form, the effects of wear on these historic artworks.

Acknowledgements

Many thanks to Dr Jeff Oliver, Department of Archeology, University of Aberdeen for his time, patience and advice. Thanks to Alison Kennedy for taking time to look at the census records and for providing me with the primary source material. Also, for helping to collect stories concerning some of the names discussed. Also thanks to all my friends who have supported me by coming up the Mither Tap and helping record the carvings. Lastly, Jan in the Bennachie Centre for letting me store my equipment when required.

REFERENCES

Beaton, H.   1915   At the Back of Bennachie.
                            (Also, Abdn. Uni. Special Coll., MS 3477.)

Carter, I.   1979   Farm life in Northeast Scotland 1840-1914. The Poor
                            Man's Country, Glasgow.

Champion, M. 2015   Medieval Graffiti, London.

Crang, M.   1997   *"Picturing Practices: Research Through the Tourist Gaze"*,
                            in Progress in Human Geography, 21, 3, 359-373.

Donnelly, T.   1975   The Development of the Aberdeen Granite Industry
                            1750 - 1939. unpublished PhD thesis, University
                            of Aberdeen. (Published 1989)

Evans, A.K.B. 2003   The Impact of the Railway on Society in Britain, Aldershot.

Fagen, J.   2011   The Bennachie Colony Project: Examining the Lives
                            and Impact of the Bennachie Colonists, Chapel of Garioch.

Ferrell, J.   1993   Crimes of Style Urban Graffiti and the Politics of
                            Criminality, New York.

Frederick, U. 2014   *"Signs of the times: Archaeological approaches to*
and Clarke A.   *historical and contemporary graffiti"*, in Australian
                            Archaeology, 78, 54-57.

Glendening, J. 1997   The High Road: Romantic Tourism, Scotland and
                            Literature, London.

Historic Scotland	2015	Maeshowe and the heart of Neolithic Orkney, Historic Scotland Official Souvenir Guide.
James, A.	1983	"Agriculture in Aberdeenshire in the Eighteen Sixties", in Whiteley, A.W.M. (ed.) Bennachie Again, Chapel of Garioch, 54-63.
Keegan P.	2006	Writing and Drawing on the Walls of Pompeii: How the study of graffiti relates to the HSC Ancient History Core Syllabus for 2006.
Kennedy, A.	2018	Email from Alison Kennedy.
McConnochie, A.I.	1890	Bennachie, Aberdeen.
Major, S.	2015	Early Victorian Railway Excursions: The Million go Forth, Barnsley.
Milne, J.	1947	Twixt Ury and Don and Round About, Inverurie.
Oliver, J., Armstrong, J., Milek, K., Schofield, J. Edward, Gould, A. & Noble, G.	2016	"The Bennachie Colony: A Nineteenth-Century Informal Community in Northeast Scotland", in International Journal of Historical Archaeology, 20, 2, 341-377.
Oliver, J. & Neal, T. (eds.)	2010	Wild Signs: Graffiti in Archaeology and History, in Studies in Contemporary and Historical Archaeology, 6, Oxford.
Oliver, J. & Neal T.	2010	"Elbow Grease and Time to Spare: The Place of Tree Carving", in: Oliver, J. and Neal, T. (eds.), 15-22.
Ransom, P.J.G	2007	The Iron Road: The Railway in Scotland, Edinburgh.
RCAHMS	2011	A Practical Guide to Recording Archaeological Sites, Edinburgh

Sanz, I.D.   2014   *"Rock Art Recording Methods: From Traditional*
                        to Digital", in The Archaeological Record, 6351-6357.

Sanz, I.D.,   2013   *"Latest Developments in Rock Art Recording: Towards*
Villaverde, V.,   *an Integral Documentation of Levantine Rock Art*
Lopez-Montalvo, E.,   *Sites Combining 2D and 3D Recording Techniques"*,
Lerma, J.L. &   in Journal of Archaeological Science, 40, 1879–1889.
Cabrelles, M.

Sharp, K.,   2008   The Prehistoric Rock Art of England: Recording,
Barnett, T. &   Managing and Enjoying our Carved Heritage,
Rushton, S.   Newcastle Upon Tyne.

Turnock, D.   1977   *Stages of Agricultural Improvement in the Uplands*
                        of Scotland's Grampian Region", in Journal of
                        Historical Geography, 3, 4, 327-347.

Urry, J.   1992   *"The Tourist Gaze 'Revisited'"*, in American
                        Behavioural Scientist, 36, 2, 172-186

Watson, A.   1999   Oyne Past and Present, Coupar.

Whiteley,   1976   The Book of Bennachie, Coupar.
A.W.M.(ed.)

Whiteley,   1983   Bennachie Again, Coupar.
A.W.M.(ed.)

Wood, S.   1985   The Shaping of 19th-Century Aberdeenshire, Stevenage.

PITTODRIE BEDE HOUSE ARCHIVAL RESEARCH

Colin H. Miller

INTRODUCTION

The Bede House is located at the foot of Bennachie, at grid reference NJ 693235, 0.4 ml. (0.6 km.), southwest of Pittodrie House and just west of the ancient highway known as the Old Aberdeen Turnpike.

The most accessible account of the Bede House is to be found in A.I. McConnochie's 'Bennachie', as noted below. The authoritative online database, Canmore, gives limited descriptions, but no systematic history or chronology of the Bede House has come to light. This information gap invited further investigation. The process began without any clear idea of what questions to ask, and where the answers might be found. The questions soon emerged; the answers took a little longer, and some remain to reveal themselves!

As with an archaeological dig, the archival research started with recent material and attempted to trace its antecedents, linking back where possible to earlier and earlier sources. This paper thus attempts to trace the 'golden thread' of references to Pittodrie's Bede House back through time. The results of this investigation are then presented as a conventional timeline of events starting with the earliest available reference. As the pitfalls and high points of the quest may also be of interest, these are recounted towards the end of the paper.

SOME QUESTIONS

The meaning of 'bede house'. The term derives from 'beadsmen', a pre-Reformation designation for indigents who received alms and accommodation from a benefactor. According to Catholic belief, when the time came, such good works would speed the benefactor's progress through purgatory and subsequent elevation to heaven. In return, the beneficiaries were duty-bound to pray for the soul of their sponsor (McAleese, 2012).

The concept at Pittodrie. In Scotland, bede houses and similar establishments certainly existed in the 16th-century, and probably earlier, as evidenced by the setting up, in 1581, of a Commission of the Scottish Parliament tasked with reforming their administration, which seems to have been suffering from misdirection, "under colour of reformation of the religion" (RPS [Records of the Parliament of Scotland], 1581/10/36).

However, while the possibility of an earlier establishment cannot be ruled out, it appears that the Erskines of Pittodrie established their Bede House c.1640. The 17th-century attitude towards the deserving poor can be inferred from the opinion of the kirk session of the parish of Oyne, who intimated in 1687 that, "those who are really indigent [as distinct from beggars and vagabonds] be maintained within their own respective parishes to whom they belong" (Mitchell, 1825, 451).

The occupants of the Pittodrie Bede House had a duty of Sunday worship in the presence of their benefactor, the laird of Pittodrie, whose lands included parts of the parishes of Oyne and Chapel of Garioch. As the available evidence shows that in this case the arrangement was initiated well after the Reformation, it should be noted that the terms 'bede house' and 'bedesmen' are anachronistic, although they clearly remained in popular use. In a literal sense the correct terminology might be 'almshouse' and 'almsmen', but this does not seem to have been applied in this instance.

The exact location of Pittodrie's Bede House. Given the presence of field and documentary evidence of a variety of buildings and enclosure features in the general vicinity of the site, the question arose as to whether the building so named on Ordnance Survey (OS) mapping was in fact the actual bede house. This doubt was effectively dispelled by the results of the archival and archaeological investigations (see Ralston & Shepherd, this volume). However, the possibility of other structures in the vicinity having had this purpose at an earlier date remains as a valid question, to which the answer will depend on any further archaeological and archival discoveries should they be forthcoming.

Sources of information. The absence of a structured history of Pittodrie Estate left the field wide open for the researcher willing to explore uncharted waters. A variety of 19th-century mapping and antiquarian publications gave tantalising clues; while a small collection of 18th-century family papers held at the University of Aberdeen's Special Collections Centre (SCC) left occasional but distinct footprints on the archival trail. The above sources led ultimately to key evidence from the first half of the 17th-century, as reported below. A critical absence is the western sheet of a two-part estate plan made in 1773 by George Brown, a pupil of the noted

18th-century land surveyor Peter May. There is little doubt that this plan would have depicted the Bede House site in some detail, giving information on its layout and possibly its condition at that time.

THE GOLDEN THREAD

The bulk of this section is arranged in reverse chronological order, starting with the most recent material and tracing the core thread back through time to progressively earlier sources. As such, the process is similar to the sequence of an archaeological excavation. However, the author's archival research process was rather less systematic, and the results presented here have therefore been sorted into a suitably structured order.

It follows that the journey should start at the present day. However, in the absence of any known survival of information in the oral tradition, it is fitting to quote from A. I. McConnochie's 'Bennachie', first published in 1890, re-published by James G. Bisset Ltd. in 1985, and Scholar's Choice in 2015; and still the source of today's popular knowledge of the Bede House. The author refers (somewhat ambiguously) to

> *"…the foundations of the "Bede House", or houses, rather, for there are said to have been several of them, very small, each with its own little "yardie".* (McConnochie, 1890, 27)

Current large-scale Ordnance Survey (OS) mapping labels the site as 'Bede House (remains of)' and depicts both the outline of the building and the boundaries of its yard, probably derived from 1973 surveying. Other than the place name and a conventional symbol, these features had been absent from successive OS editions after initially appearing on the 19th-century 1st Edition, surveyed in 1866-67, where a roofless building is shown with an associated sub-rectangular enclosure or yard (Ordnance Survey, 1868). Extensive robbing of stone for other purposes has taken place in the area, and it is probable that this has occurred both before and after the 1860s survey. The result has been progressive loss of visibility of the features, exacerbated by vegetation growth and subsequent tree-planting.

A LiDAR survey carried out in 2013 (under the auspices of the University of Aberdeen, Aberdeenshire Council and Forestry Commission Scotland) revealed the footings of the 'Bede House' and related stone dykes, more or less as depicted on the First Edition OS map. The OS has never recorded certain features to the east of the Old Aberdeen Turnpike, which are revealed by the LiDAR survey, and which may possibly explain McConnochie's tantalising reference to the possibility of there being more than one bede house. The features in question were presumably too residual in nature to be worthy of record by the OS, even at the time of the first survey.

The record on the Canmore website gives the results of a 2002 survey by RCAHMS. Their measurements and description, while clearly the result of their own fieldwork, are consistent with the OS report of 1973 reported below. There is one significant extra detail - the mention of a trackway onto which the building's entrance-way opens (Historic Environment Scotland [HES], ?2002), a detail to which this paper will return in due course.

In 1973, as subsequently reported on the Canmore database [*ibid*.], site visits and surveys by the OS recorded a

> *"rectangular building … [with] a double entrance on its E side, one on either side of a central division … situated at the E side of a sub-rectangular enclosure … The entrance to the enclosure is in the E, opposite to and connected to the entrance to the house".*

The core text of the entry in the Aberdeenshire Sites and Monuments Record (Aberdeenshire Council, 1997) is apparently based on the above report.

Thanks to tree-felling in the immediate vicinity, a 1973 aerial photograph (Bailies of Bennachie Archives, 1973, 12/1-85, print no. 203) shows the Bede House, its yard and traces of the 'Robertson Highway' (of probable 18th-century date - see below) passing the entrance.

In the absence of any known earlier 20th-century sources, it is now necessary to revisit McConnochie's account in 'Bennachie', which stated that the Bede House:

> *"…entertained four poor men, who were entitled to a peck of meal, and half-a-peck of malt each, per week, and who had to wear livery gowns, and to walk to church on Sundays before the [Pittodrie] family".*
> *"The last inmates were two women".* (McConnochie, 1890, 27)

No source is given for this quite detailed information. Perhaps McConnochie thought it unnecessary to reference his sources in what was essentially an in-depth guidebook for Bennachie. It does however pose an intriguing lure for the archival researcher.

McConnochie's book itself has no illustration of the Bede House, and in passing it should be noted that neither the George Washington Wilson collection nor the Cormack archive of 19th-century local photographs contain images of the Bede House site, which might otherwise have portrayed the scene as surveyed by the OS at the time. Clearly, however, there was enough surviving stonework to justify depicting the walls of the building and related enclosure dykes on the First Edition OS mapping.

In 1878, twelve years before 'Bennachie' appeared, 'Inverurie and the Earldom of the Garioch' was published. This comprised the antiquarian researches of the Reverend John Davidson, Minister of Inverurie, and it provides several clues. Davidson states that the Erskines acquired 'the lands of Balehagirdy' in 1357 (Davidson, 1878, 63). He records that a 'Hospital of Balhaggarty' was authorised by the General Assembly of the Church of Scotland (*ibid.*, 156) and was ratified by an act of the Scottish Parliament (*ibid.*, 147). Quoting from an earlier document, Davidson notes that the building consisted of, "two chambers and one mid-room" and was linked with the Chapel of the Garioch (*ibid.*, 156). Furthermore, in the 17th-century, the Erskines began to designate themselves as "of Pittodrie" (*ibid.*, 418), and "An hospital at Pittodrie" (*ibid.*, 81) is described in terms which match the above quotation from McConnochie, word for word. Davidson's text (*ibid.*, 156) makes it clear that he interpreted the hospitals of Balhaggarty and Pittodrie to be one and the same entity.

The Name Books compiled by the OS during their preparation of the first edition mapping in the mid-19th century provide a unique record of local knowledge supporting many of the place-names on today's maps. For 'Bede House', also spelled 'Bead House', the Name Book produced in 1865-71 (Ordnance Survey 1865-71, ref. OS1/1/70/75) states that

> *"Nothing but a trace of this building remains. Its date of erection is not known, but proprietors at that time having to support the poor of the district, this house was built for the Pitcaple district, and four or five men were said to have been kept in it".*

Since this data is directly linked to the feature on the OS map, any doubt about the sometime function of that specific building is more or less eliminated. The authorities for the information were Colonel H.K. Erskine (the landowner, and therefore deemed to be a reliable source) and a Mr. C. Watt. Although McConnochie refers to the latter as having been something of a local character, there is good reason to trust Watt's testimony. The author is indebted to Alison Kennedy for information from successive census returns from 1841 to 1871 which record his name as occupant of Craigwell, a crofthouse adjacent to the Bede House site. The 1841 census also shows his mother, aged 86, at Craigwell, while in 1771

Bede House entrance and south chamber.
"It consists of two chambers and one mid-room". (Spalding Club, 1843, 527)
From bottom left, the photo shows the approach pathway, the triangular threshold stone with adjacent checked and drilled stone for main door, and (left of orange peg) threshold and checked stone for door of one of the "two chambers". The peg is in the "mid-room" space, and the north chamber is out of shot to the right. (Photo: C.H. Miller)

the Pittodrie rental estimate (SCC, 1771, 27) shows that Craigwell was tenanted by a George Watt. This strongly suggests that the Watt family lore stretched back at least to times when an occupied Bede House would have been fresh in the memory.

Prior to the arrival of the OS on the scene, a plan of the Commonty of Bennachie was prepared by Alexander Smith (Smith, 1845). The Bede House is named, and shown as being situated on Pittodrie land just outwith the Commonty boundary and in the general locality of the site in question. There is insufficient detail to determine if the building had a roof at that time.

The material revealed thus far seems to authenticate that the Bede House existed and that it was on the site depicted by the OS. However, as Davidson's information was derived either from historic records, or from earlier compilations, it is necessary to look further back in time.

Fortunately for the progress of this research, in 1843, the Spalding Club - an Aberdeen-based antiquarian society - published Volume 1 of their 'Collections'. Therein can be found the information and, in some cases, the exact wording subsequently cited by Davidson and McConnochie in describing the Bede House, and to which one or both of those authors may well have had access. The Spalding Club description, in full, is as follows:

> *"There was an HOSPITAL, at Pittodrie, for four poor men, (founded under King Charles II. by William Erskin of Pittodrie,) who ought to have each one peck of meal, and half a peck of malt, weekly; to wear livery gowns, and go to the church on Sundays before the family. It consists of two chambers and one mid-room".*
> (Spalding Club, 1843, 527)

There is no specific indication of the source of the information. However, the Editor's Preface (*ibid.*, xi) suggests that it was among material in the 'View of the Diocese of Aberdeen', which the Spalding Club 'printed from a manuscript in the Library of the Faculty of Advocates at Edinburgh' referenced as 'MSS. Bibl. Adv. 31. 2. 12. (Jac. V. 6. 24.)', and which forms a large proportion of the contents of Volume 1. The 'View' seems to have been an unfinished collection compiled by 'Al. Keith', a zealous presbyter of the Episcopal Church of Scotland. Although deemed to be unfinished, it is noted on the Edinburgh copy as having been completed on 25 November 1732 (though retaining missing entries within some of the parish entries). A handwritten marginal note in the SCC copy of the Spalding club volume indicates that Keith was an MA of Marischal College and the Episcopal Minister of the [Aberdeenshire] parish of Cruden.

Assuming the Bede House information to be derived as inferred above, this is something of a breakthrough - a tenable link to more than a century earlier. The Spalding text, "There was an HOSPITAL (etc.)" would appear to be of 18th-century origin, rather than from the 1840s, which suggests that it is quoted from 'View of the Diocese' and therefore implying that by 1732 the Bede House had ceased to function as such. Be that as it may, the text strongly underpins the 19th-century accounts, taking the investigation back to a time when the Bede House must have been of recent memory and some 40 years before the 1771 record of George Watt's tenancy at Craigwell.

Also in Volume 1 of the 'Collections' is an explanation of the potential confusion between the names Balhaggarty and Pittodrie – thus (*ibid.*, lxxv & 532):

"'Pittodrie, the seat of Erskin of Pittodrie, descended of Sir [Thomas] Erskin of Brechin, (a cadet of Dun,) secretary to King James V. He exchanged, (very surprisingly,) the estate of Brechin with the Earl of Mar, (who is said to have been his nephew,) for that of Pittodrie, (then called the estate of Balhaggartie, ... ')"

Before further excursions into the 18th-century, two early 19th-century maps enter the picture - Thomson's 'Atlas' of 1832, and Robertson's map of 1822. Thomson's Aberdeenshire map appears to be based on the Robertson map, so it is the latter which provides the earlier depiction of a road linking Pittodrie and the Garioch with Donside (Robertson, 1822). This strategic link with Donside - termed by the present author, for convenience, the 'Robertson Highway' - skirts the southeastern and southern slopes of Bennachie, and must be the 'trackway' passing the Bede House entrance referred to in the 2002 RCAHMS survey (see also Ralston & Shepherd, this volume, figure 28). Indeed, the line of the road at this point can be traced today, both on LiDAR and as a faint profile on the ground. The road's junction with the 'Old Aberdeen Turnpike' is cut by the dyke, of unknown date, bordering the west side of the Turnpike. Since the road was not shown on the 1st-edition OS map, surveyed in 1866-67, it must be assumed that by then it had ceased to be readily apparent. It may indeed have been subsumed in woodland planting by that time.

We now turn to the 18th-century when, at some date, it seems likely that the Pittodrie Bede House ceased to be used for its intended purpose. Comparisons with other similar north-east establishments are of interest. We learn that by 1732 the 'Beidsmen's' house at Tarves, "... is slated, is neglected and quite waste" (Simpson, 1938, 249) while by 1735 the minister reports "the roof off, the furniture gone, and the yard misapplied" (*ibid.*). At a later date, decay must have affected the bede house at Rathven, near Buckie, which was still extant in the 19th-century and was reported in the 1840s to have been recently repaired (NSA, 268).

A fortunate archival resource is the 'Survey and Rental' of Pittodrie Estate, dated 1771, held at SCC (SCC, 1771). This appears to have been compiled by George Brown, land surveyor, who was responsible for the two associated plans. The document is a bound volume listing estimated rentals for each of the crofts, farms, etc. on the estate, and also including parcels not subject to rental, such as the estate woodlands. The absence of a specific record for the Bede House and its yard suggests that it was no longer a separate physical and functional entity, although the possibility that it was engrossed in the catch-all 'houses, yards, roads' category cannot be ruled out[1]. However, there are references to 'Beidhouse park' and 'the Beid', which confirm the continuing use of the place-name at that time.

George Brown's survey resulted in the production in 1773 of a large scale plan of the estate. This might have been expected to provide a clear snapshot of the Bede House site, whatever its state of ongoing use or abandonment, at the time of the survey. The plan comprised two sheets, one presenting the eastern half of the estate, the other the western half. Unfortunately, while the east sheet has survived and is readily accessible at SCC (SCC, 1773), the western sheet, encompassing the vicinity of the Bede House, remains elusive. References to the plan in 'Peter May Land Surveyor' (SHS, 1979, xxxiv) link it with work for 'Lord Forbes at Pittodrie', but this seems unlikely, and there is perhaps scope for confusion here. The laird of Pittodrie at the time was an Erskine, not a Forbes; while Lord Forbes himself was at 'Putachie' (now Castle Forbes). In passing, one might observe that 'Putachie' and 'Pittodrie' are place-names which might easily become confused. Even if the plan did find its way to Putachie, an early 19th-century fire at Castle Forbes destroyed much of the family's archives (Shepherd, 2018). Also, Pittodrie Estate changed hands on two significant occasions after the tenure of the Erskines, with accompanying potential for dispersal or loss of records.

Despite the lack of the 1773 plan, it was possible to extend the research further back in time. The papers of the Erskine family of Pittodrie, held at SCC, include some 18th-century references of particular interest. A draft marriage contract of 1779 (SCC, 1779, 5-6) refers to

> *"the right of Patronage and Superiority of the Hospital of Balhaggarty, which of old was the patronage of the Chaplainries of the Chappel of Garioch, Wartle, Colliehill, Pitgavenny and Kirkinglass, now erected into the said Hospital called the Hospital of Balhaggarty by virtue of an Act of the General Assembly of the Church of Scotland, And Conform to Act of Parliament holden at Edinburgh the seventeenth day of November 1641 years lying within the parishes of Inverury, Raine and Bourty and Sherriffdom of Aberdeen ..."*

As it is understood that Balhaggarty and Pittodrie are successive names for the same estate, it can reasonably be assumed that the 'Hospital' in question is the Pittodrie Bede House, despite the somewhat confusing parish references. The significance of this document is that it contains primary evidence of the founding

---

1   *Though, as a charitable institution maintained by the laird, it might also not have been necessarily liable to a rentable value.*

of the 'Hospital' in accordance with Acts of the General Assembly of the Church of Scotland and of the Parliament of Scotland.

The text quoted above, with variations, appears earlier in the Pittodrie papers, in a 1751 Bond of Tailzie (SCC, 1751, 3-4). One may speculate that this somewhat standard description has itself been copied from earlier documents. The 1751 wording incorrectly gives the date of the act of parliament as 16th November 1641.

The 18th-century Erskine papers thus pointed a further century back in time, and perhaps to the very beginning of the story of the Bede House. The archival research therefore moved to the records of the Scottish Parliament and the General Assembly.

Thanks to the University of St Andrews, the Act of Parliament dated 17/11/1641 can readily be found on the website www.rps.ac.uk which contains the records of the Parliaments of Scotland to 1707. The following extract (RPS, 1641) from the translated version of the Act, shows that Thomas Erskine was anxious to ratify the use of funds from historic chaplainries to provide for the occupants of the Bede House:

> "which whole chaplainries and lands thereto mortified had been of a long time since feued by the chaplains to the heritors for small feu duties, so that there remained but one very final duty to be paid yearly out of these whole lands, and the said Thomas as patron being most willing that the small duties yet remaining might be employed to some pious use had upon his own charges and expenses erected and built a house of two houses height at the Chapel of Garioch, of intention to put some old, poor and decrepit men therein for their better accommodation of their service to God, which intention of his could not so well be put in execution unless these small duties yet remaining of these chaplainries were a part of their provision and maintenance; and seeing the said Thomas had the right of patronage and also that there was no use for the said small duties according to their first foundation, therefore he, as patron foresaid, thought it fit to alter the said foundation and confer the same to these poor men for their better maintenance, to which he did most humbly supplicate the approbation of the foresaid general assembly so far as did concern the ecclesiastic part, and from the same assembly be represented to this present parliament, whereby the civil and legal authority might be interposed, and that the said late erected house might be called the Hospital of the Barony of Balhalgardy in all

time coming, which supplication and desire thereof being seen
and considered by the said general assembly and found the same to
be reasonable, they referred the same to this present parliament, as
the extract of an act of the same assembly of the date at Edinburgh,
29 August 1639 foresaid, at more length bears".

The actual structure of the building is stated above, as being 'of two houses height', while the original Scots text (*ibid.*) is "of tua house heighte". It is possible to infer a subtle difference in meaning between the translated and the original Scots versions, namely, that the building was either of two storeys, or alternatively of one storey of considerable height (which could arguably include loft accommodation). Descriptions elsewhere of the building having, "two chambers and one mid-room" would be consistent with a single-storey dwelling but would imply that each chamber would be shared by two men (unless any loft accommodation was similarly divided), whereas a two storey building would presumably have four chambers. Certainly the archaeological evidence hints at there being some 'upstairs' accommodation, as reported elsewhere in this volume.

The text of the 1641 Act ties the 'Hospital of the Barony of Balhalgardy' with a location 'at the Chapel of Garioch'. As far as the author is aware there is no record of any comparable 17th-century institution at the settlement of Chapel of Garioch itself, while Pittodrie's Bede House is at only 1.5 miles' distance. It therefore seems reasonable to conclude that the act of parliament concerns the so-called Bede House forming the subject of this paper.

1641 is not quite the earliest involvement of the Scottish Parliament with the Bede House. On 1st October 1639, presumably as a necessary preliminary to the drafting of the Act itself, Thomas Erskine had presented a supplication to the parliamentary commission for plantation of kirks (RPS, 1639), recorded as

"Item, the reference and supplicatione presented by the Laird of
Pittodrie for erectioune of the hospitall of Balhaggardie".

The 1641 Act also records that on 29th August 1639 Thomas Erskine had secured the approval of the General Assembly of the Church of Scotland for the use of chaplainry funds to establish the 'Hospital'. This is an interesting example of the absorption of chaplainry arrangements in post-Reformation Scotland when their original purpose had ceased to be recognised. Meanwhile, for the archival researcher, the text provides a date for the assembly's deliberation on Thomas Erskine's proposal. Summary records of the acts of the General Assembly for 1639 have been digitised as images on the 'Virtual Volumes' facility at the National

Records of Scotland, but the author could find no mention of the Hospital. In the relevant document - CH 1/1/4 Register of the General Assembly at Glasgow, 1638 and Edinburgh, 1639 - what appears to be standardised secretarial terminology refers to, "A number of particular bills not needful here to be [?imparted]" (NRS, 1639, 264-5). Thus, the possible explanation of the omission is that the topic of the Hospital was of too localised a nature to be included (except, presumably, in the Minutes, which unfortunately are no longer extant (NRS, 2018). Therefore, the earliest surviving record of the Bede House may prove to be Thomas Erskine's 1639 supplication, as cited above.

Bede House Timeline

Based on the above material and archaeological evidence, the following chronology can be compiled:

1639 (29 August): Hospital of the Barony of Balhalgardy (i.e. the Bede House) "erected" by virtue of an Act of the General Assembly of the Church of Scotland.

1639 (1 October): Thomas Erskine submits a supplication to a parliamentary commission regarding the 'Hospital'.

1639-1641? Assumed date of construction of 'Hospital' by Thomas Erskine.

1641 (17 November): Parliament of Scotland ratifies Erskine's use of former chaplainry revenue for maintenance of occupants of Bede House.

18th-century? Bede House, or at least its use for its original purpose, likely to have become defunct (based on absence of specific entry in 1771 estate record). However, the 1779 draft marriage contract (*op. cit.*) notes that the Erskines retain "the right of Patronage and Superiority of the Hospital of Balhaggarty".

18th-19th century: Robbing of stonework from house and dykes.

Late 19th-century - early 20th-century: Tree planting in yard.

20th-century (?c1970): Felling of above timber crop.

20th-century (?1970s): Tree planting in yard and building.

2018: Archaeological excavation (partial) of Bede House and yard dykes.

2019: At the time of writing, tree felling in yard and building is scheduled for spring 2019, and will be subject to protection of archaeological features.

THE QUEST

It is never possible to be completely methodical when conducting archival research. A brutalist approach might restrict itself to the relentless use of search engines, to the detriment of any kind of enjoyment to be derived from the quest. The author is not entirely embarrassed to admit to a somewhat haphazard process of exploration in such directions as happened to present themselves. As one proceeds on such a course, shortcomings in the process and gaps in the results tend to make their presence known. Unexpected sources appear, and the research leads off into new directions. That the results in this case cohere into something of a history of the Bede House is fortunate, and owes much to debate with other members of the archaeology team, assisted by a goodly measure of luck.

Some of the pitfalls and rewards experienced during the research are recounted here, in the same sequence as 'The Golden Thread' above, in the hope that this will be of benefit to other researchers. An over-arching feature is the wide-ranging availability of data online, enabling information to be rapidly acquired and compared.

McConnochie's 'Bennachie' provides the most accessible account. It was rewarding to trace the author's text back to previous sources, but frustrating that no source was provided or discovered for his references to the last occupants being two women and to there having been several bede houses (McConnochie, *op.cit.*). One may surmise that these came from oral tradition which has since been lost with the passage of time. On a positive note, census information, the OS Name Book and estate papers (the 1771 Pittodrie rental volume), proved invaluable in cross-referencing with McConnochie's reference to Charles Watt.

Davidson's 'Inverurie and the Earldom of the Garioch' revealed the origins of the Bede House by linking its founding (as the 'Hospital of Balhaggarty') with deliberations in the General Assembly of the Church of Scotland and the Parliament of Scotland. Notably, however, Davidson erroneously gave the year of the act of parliament as 1651 when in fact it was 1641. Ironically, this particular detail sent this researcher back to check the material on www.rps.ac.uk . Of the two Erskine family papers, the 1779 draft marriage contract gives the date as 17th November 1641, while the 1751 bond of tailzie gives it as 16th November 1641. Naturally, one would assume that the earlier document would be the correct version, and indeed on browsing the rps website an act of 16/11/1641 was found which implied that any obligations formerly imposed by the (excommunicated Roman Catholic) bishops would continue but under the aegis of the monarchy. Assuming that such obligations might include those pertaining to bede houses, the author accepted this somewhat disappointing result, until the fortunate discovery of Davidson's error and the discovery of the Hospital of Balhalgardy act of parliament with its correct date of 17/11/1641. It must be admitted that a search on the RPS site using the term 'Pittodrie' would have instantly revealed not only the act of parliament, but also Thomas Erskine's supplication to the Scottish Parliament of 1639 which had not been mentioned in other sources.

The Spalding Club 'Collections' published in 1843 provided much the same information as Davidson's subsequent work, but with the rewarding note that the information could have been originally set down in 1732 - thus affording the researcher a great leap further back in time, although with the minor aberration that the founding of the 'Hospital' is credited to William Erskine, rather than Thomas, which contradicts the 17th-century parliamentary records.

Finally, one must record the intervention of Sod's Law in that the all-important western sheet of the 1773 Pittodrie estate plan appears to be missing - if only in the hope that somewhere, sometime it will turn up!

Archives and Archaeology

As a participant in the 2018 dig, the author was able to observe instances where the archival information informed the field excavation and vice versa. Notably, the documentary sources seem to confirm that the building under excavation was indeed the Bede House. Practical examples include the references to the internal ground plan, the possibility of a two-storey (or tall) structure, and the map evidence for the 'Robertson Highway' all of which are reflected in archaeological observations on the site. This synchrony stimulated ongoing discussion and questioning which benefitted both processes and generally assisted in maintaining team spirit.

Sources

Aberdeenshire Council, 1997, Aberdeenshire Sites and Monuments Record - NJ62SE0003 - Bede House, Aberdeenshire Council. (https://online.aberdeenshire. gov.uk/smrpub/default.aspx)

Bailies of Bennachie Archives, 1973 to date, ref. 12/1-85. Aerial photography flown 21 August 1973; print no. 203. Contact: info@bailiesofbennachie.co.uk

Historic Environment Scotland, ?2002. Canmore National Record of the Historic Environment - Bedehouse Wood, Historic Environment Scotland. (https://canmore.org.uk/site/18183/bedehouse-wood)

NRS, 1639. Register of the General Assembly at Glasgow, 1638 and Edinburgh 1639. Held at National Records of Scotland, ref CH 1/1/4.

NRS, 2018. E-mail from onlineresources@nrscotland.gov.uk to Miller, C. 11 September.

NSA - Gordon, J., ed. The New Statistical Account of Scotland / by the ministers of the respective parishes, under the superintendence of a committee of the Society for the Benefit of the Sons and Daughters of the Clergy. Rathven, Banff, Vol. 13, Edinburgh, Blackwoods and Sons, 1845. (http://stataccscot.edina.ac.uk/link/nsa-vol13-p245-parish-banff-rathven)

Ordnance Survey, Aberdeenshire LIV.1 (Oyne) [25 inch to the mile], 1st edition, Ordnance Survey, GB, 1868. NLS Map images. (https://maps.nls.uk/view/74425406)

Ordnance Survey, Name Book - Aberdeenshire - Parish of Oyne, 1865-71. (https://scotlandsplaces.gov.uk/digital-volumes/ordnance-survey-name-books/aberdeenshire-os-name-books-1865-1871/aberdeenshire-volume-70)

RPS, 1639. The Records of the Parliaments of Scotland to 1707, K.M. Brown *et al* eds. (St Andrews, 2007-2019), Supplications remitted to commission for plantation of kirks… . Ref C1639/8/38. (http://www.rps.ac.uk)

RPS, 1641. The Records of the Parliaments of Scotland to 1707, K.M. Brown *et al* eds. (St Andrews, 2007-2019), Act regarding the erection of the hospital of Balhalgardy. Ref. 1641/8/380. (http://www.rps.ac.uk)

Robertson, James, 1822. Topographical and military map of the counties of Aberdeen, Banff and Kincardine, London. Using NLS Map images. (https://maps.nls.uk/view/74400182)

SCC, 1751. Scroll Disposition and Bond of Taillzie Thos. Erskine of Pitodry To Himself & heirs of Taillzie within specified 1751 Held at University of Aberdeen Special Collections Centre (SCC), ref MS 2524/3.

SCC, 1771. Contents Measures and Estimates of the Lands and Barrony of Pittodery lying in the Parishes of Oyne, and Chappell of Girrioch, taken from a survey made 1771. Unpublished volume, held at University of Aberdeen Special Collections Centre (SCC), ref MS 2392.

SCC, 1773. Records of F.A. MacDonald and Partners, engineers and surveyors (incorporating Walker & Duncan, Aberdeen): maps and plans collection – item no. 5501. Held at University of Aberdeen Special Collections Centre (SCC), ref MS 3860.

SCC, 1779. Draught Contract of Marriage Betwixt Major Henry Knight And Miss Mary Erskine 1779. Held at University of Aberdeen Special Collections Centre (SCC), ref MS 2524/8.

SHS, 1979. Adams, Ian H. ed. Papers on Peter May Land Surveyor 1749-1793. Edinburgh: Scottish History Society.

Smith, Alexander, 1845. Reduced Plan of the Common of Bein-na-chie. Glasgow. Held at University of Aberdeen Special Collections Centre (SCC), ref MS 2769-I-32-1.

Spalding Club, 1843. Collections for a History of the Shires of Aberdeen and Banff, Vol. I . Aberdeen, Spalding Club.

REFERENCES

Davidson, Rev. J.	1878	Inverurie and the Earldom of the Garioch - A Topographical and Historical Account of the Garioch from the Earliest Time to the Resolution Settlement, Aberdeen, A. Brown & Co. (https://archive.org/details/inverurieearldom00davi/page/n8)
McAleese, R.	2012	"Aberdeen's Bedesmen - poverty and piety", in History Scotland, January/February 2012.
McConnochie, A.I.	1890	Bennachie, Aberdeen: D. Wyllie & Son. (https://ia802707.us.archive.org/17/items/bennachie00mccogoog/bennachie00mccogoog.pdf)

Mitchell, J.   1825.   The Scotsman's Library; Being a Collection of
                        Anecdotes and Facts Illustrative of Scotland and
                        Scotsmen, June, 1825, Edinburgh, J. Anderson jun.
                        (https://archive.org/details/scotsmanslibrar00mitcgoog/)

Shepherd, C.   2018   E-mail to Miller, C. 15 June.

Simpson, W.   1938   *"Tolquhon Castle and its Builder"*, in Proceedings of the
                        Society of Antiquaries of Scotland, 72, 248-272.
                        (http://journals.socantscot.org/index.php/psas/article/view/8076).

THE PITTODRIE ESTATE 'BEDE HOUSE' EXCAVATIONS

Iain Ralston and Colin Shepherd

INTRODUCTION

The Bennachie 'Bede House' has for a long time been known simply as a spot on the map and accepted uncritically as a local charitable residence for poor people of long ago. Once the evidence is considered, however, its history can clearly be seen to be more complicated and, at times, highly ambiguous. In 2017 the Bailies decided that the time was ripe for a determined assault on the evidence in order to try to sort fact from 'received wisdom'. A three-pronged assault included a consideration of the documentary, social and archaeological evidence. Colin Miller's paper in this publication deals with the documentary evidence whilst the social and archaeological data is assessed here.

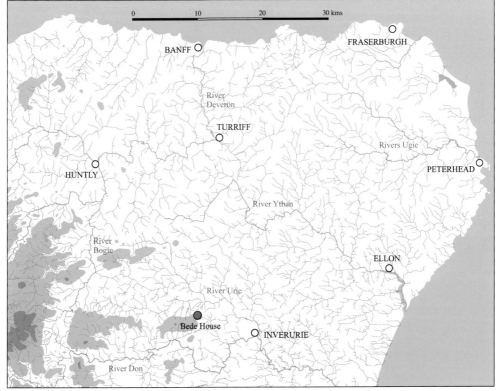

Figure 1. Location of the Pittodrie Bede House.

THE ARCHAEOLOGICAL ASSESSMENT

Iain Ralston

BACKGROUND

In Alexander McConnochie's book titled 'Bennachie' (1890, 27) he writes: *"... a little above which may be seen the foundations of the "Bede House", or houses rather, for there are said to have been several of them, very small, each with its own little "yardie"'.* The 'Bede House', as shown on the 1st edition Ordnance Survey, is situated within 'Bedehouse Wood', south-west of Pittodrie House on the east side of Bennachie at co-ordinates NJ 6933 2356.

Locating the Bede House on the ground was aided by using the 'dry-stane' dykes that are shown on the 1st edition OS map and which still stand to a considerable height in places. When first visited by the author, the site was found to exist mainly as low earthworks with only occasional stones emerging in places to suggest the possibility of walls lying beneath. McConnochie mentions these as "foundations" (*ibid*). But, prior to our fieldwork the site could easily have been walked over and missed (see Photo 1).

Photo 1. View of the 'Bede House' site before excavation.

OBJECTIVES AND METHOD

A set of aims and procedures were agreed with the Bailies and the landowner in order to attempt to understand the site and its relationship to the historical accounts previously known and recently discovered (see Miller, this volume). These 'project objectives' might be listed as:

1.   To uncover by excavation enough of the 'Bede House' structure to characterise its architecture;
2.   To produce a large scale plan of this structure and its surrounding enclosure dykes to contextualise its immediate setting;
3.   To recover dating and usage evidence;
4.   To understand the method of construction of the structural components.

Test pits were initially opened with most being expanded into trenches. In all, 15 trenches were opened across the area of the enclosure and the associated building. Key locations were targeted in the hope of gaining as much information as possible whilst limiting the extent of the interventions. Retention of data for future generations was considered an important factor to be balanced against the needs of achieving the objectives of the project. In fact, the extant archaeology proved to be much better preserved than had been considered likely. Figure 2 shows the siting of the excavation trenches and test pits as described in the text.

LOCAL GEOLOGY

This eastern end of the Bennachie/Correen ridge - the 'Bennachie Pluton' - is an igneous granitic intrusion datable to the Silurian period. Overlying this intrusion are glacial tills of the Banchory formation. Just below the site to the east lay Psammite and Semipelite rocks of the Aberdeen Formation, similarly overlain by tills of the Banchory formation (British Geological Survey online at www.mapapps.bgs.ac.uk/geologyofbritain).

Overlying the geologies, the farmlands of Pittodrie below the site are characterised as rich, brown forest soils whilst on the hillside, the site sits in a zone of competing podsols and gleys with the nitrogen-leaching podsols overlooking the stiffer gleys of the northern slopes of Bennachie (The Macaulay Institute for Soil Research, Soil Survey of Scotland, 1984). The Bede House site should be seen to conform to the fast-draining podsol zone.

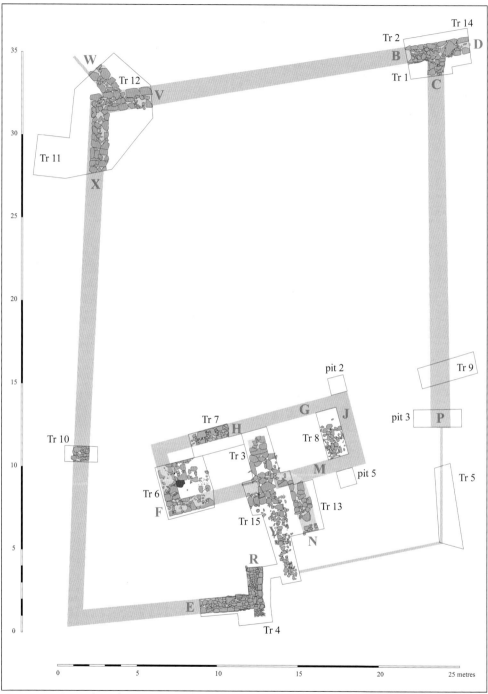

Figure 2. Site plan showing trenches, trench numbers and some feature codes.

THE EXCAVATIONS OF THE ENCLOSURE DYKES

Trench 1

The dykes that appear to delimit the Bede House enclosure were found to comprise field clearance stones. They survived in this corner as three courses of drystane construction. The dykes were found to be built directly onto the soft, natural subsoil and stood here to a maximum height of 0.85m with a width of around 0.90m. The soft natural subglacial subsoil recognised here was found to overlay a harder 'till', with this pattern recurring across the site.

It was found that dykes [B] and [C] were earlier in construction than the adjacent dyke [D]. The soil within the dykes was found to be a fine, brown loam. However, although the surviving soil level on both sides of the dyke was similar, the depth internally was greater. This may suggest deliberate management of the soils in order to create a more viable growing matrix. It suggests that subsoil may have been removed in order to deepen the garden soil or that the constant re-working and deeper digging of the garden soils created this deeper matrix. It might also suggest that the garden extended right to the dyke at this point, with no intervening path.

The small finds from this trench consist of: green bottle-glass from context (601), slate writing stylus and pot shard from (602); charcoal and pot shards from (602); incised decorated pot shard from (602).

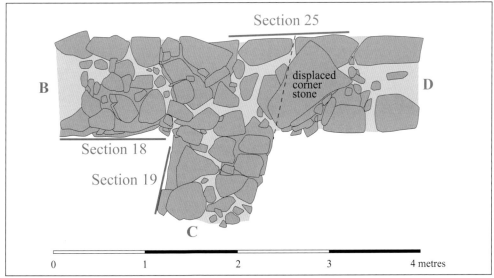

Figure 3. Plan of the intersection of features B, C and D.

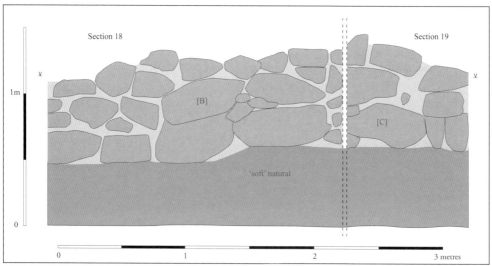

Figure 4. Sections 18 and 19.

Trenches 2 and 14

These trenches established that the relative date of dykes [B] and[C] was earlier than dyke [D] which clearly abutted [B]/[C]. As the adjoining plantation - Beid House Park - to which [D] presumably belongs, is known to have been in existence by the time of the estate survey of 1771 (MS 2392) - and probably by the time of Roy's survey in the mid 18th century - the Bede House enclosure must predate those dates. [D] had been robbed down to foundation stone level. This may have been when the plantation was subsequently enlarged (see Miller, this publication).

Section 25 shows the abutment of [D] to [B]. The 'displaced corner stone' had been slid out of position, probably during recent forestry activity. The shape of a tree root that had been forced to grow around the stone prior to its movement demonstrated unequivocally its former position.

Again, it is noteworthy that the soil to the outside of this enclosure dyke was found to be poor and very shallow in stark contrast to the garden area within the enclosure. Small finds included slate and green bottle-glass from (660).

Trench 9, Test Pit 3 and Trench 5

These interventions are considered together as each relies upon evidence from the others in order to attempt to offer a structured narrative of the observations.

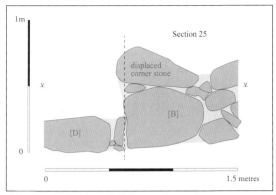

Figure 5. Section 25 (west-facing).

Trench 9 was a 1x3m trench located across the projected alignment of dyke [C]. The dyke was found to be approximately 1m in width and stood four courses high (approximately 0.95m) on its south side. However, just within the trench, the alignment was interrupted. A right angled turn on the inner face headed north. The outer face of the dyke was given a semi-circular corner rather than a hard right angle (see Photo 2). This appears to have been a well-constructed 'dog-leg' in the alignment created for some unknown purpose. Test Pit 3 was excavated to test this hypothesis. Small finds from Trench 9 was limited to some charcoal from (644).

As noted above, Test Pit 3 was excavated to prove the alignment shown in Trench 9 as well as to confirm that alignment with the remains found in Trench 5. A section of dyke, approximately 0.90m in width and surviving to no more than two stones high, was found where anticipated in line with the adjusted alignment after the dog-leg in Trench 9 (see Photo 3).

Of particular interest was the recognition of a cut [Q] and a 'fill' of yellowy-brown soil (622). This was observed in Trench 9 (Figure 6) and confirmed in this test pit. This appears to reflect an earlier raised earthen bank that predated the construction of the drystane dyke and into which the bank had been cut. A similar

Photo 2. Dog-leg in dyke alignment formed by a hard right angle internally and a rounded corner externally (on right side of picture.)

Photo 3. Test Pit 3 with re-aligned dyke.

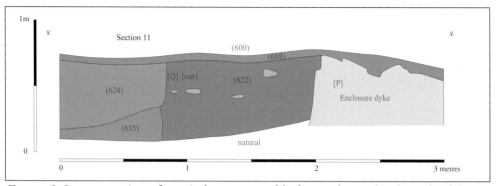

Figure 6. Section 11 (east-facing) showing possible former linear bank cut by dyke.

cut and feature was noted in Trench 12 (see below). What is strange in all three examples is that the dyke appears to have been inserted half-way across the earlier bank on its outer edge. To the south of the cut [Q], the soil was again found to be good garden loam. This seems to indicate that the garden was dug through the remains of the earlier earthen bank. Small finds noted here were window glass and pot shards from (622).

This confirmed alignment helped in the understanding of the remains in Trench 5. Initially a 1m wide trench was dug along the line of a stone scatter that was thought to have been the continuation of dyke [C]. However, the situation was not clear-cut owing to the new alignment noted above and the trench was extended several times in order to try to understand the data. The stone scatter appears to have been debris resulting from the robbing of the wall at this corner. The remains of the wall itself was discovered to lie along the new alignment.

Photo 4. The robbed remains of the dyke in Trench 5.

However, it had been comprehensively robbed and no corner to the yard was discovered (see Photo 4). The small finds from this trench consisted of green bottle-glass within (610).

Trench 12

An initial 1x1m test pit was located in the corner of dykes [V] and [X] that progressively enlarged to incorporate dyke [W]. It was noted that an apparent slight rise to the ground surface ran along an east to west axis to the south of the site. This was considered to reflect the line of the south enclosure dyke [X] covered with soil overburden. However, upon excavation it was discovered that dyke [X] lay approximately 1m further to the south than expected. Dyke [X] was found to cut into and to have followed this earthen bank. It is now thought likely that this feature could be an earlier forerunner of the drystane enclosure dykes, as noted above.

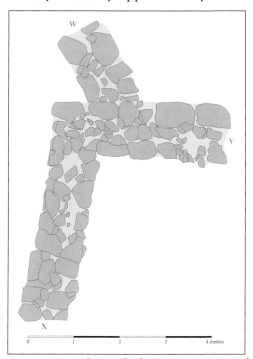

Dykes [X], [V] and [W] were found to survive to only one stone course high. Dyke [V] had a width of approximately 1.30m and dykes [X] and [W] were about 1.20m wide. All three dykes were built directly onto the soft natural subsoil. Dyke [W] is shown on the 1st Edition OS map as having a gap between it and dyke [V]. However, the excavation shows that this was not the case and that dyke [W] abuts dyke [V]. This is important as it demonstrates that [W] must post-date the construction of [V] in the same way that [D] was shown to have superseded [B]/[C] on the adjacent corner of the enclosure. Both [W] and [D], therefore, appear to be associated with the Beid House Park and utilised the pre-existing Bede House enclosure to help form one of its sides. Small finds from here consisted of slate from (636) and slate, window and green bottle-glass from (637).

Figure 7. Plan of the intersection of features V, W and X.

Trench 10

A 1x3m trench was positioned across the projected alignment of dyke [X] revealed in trench 12 further to the west. With the removal of the soil overburden

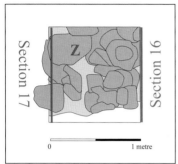
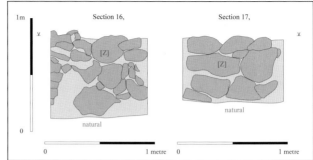

Figure 8. Plan of Trench 10 and associated sections 16 (north-facing) and 17 south-facing.

the lower courses of dyke was encountered. The dyke was constructed of field clearance stones surviving to four stone courses with a height of 0.94m and a width of approximately 1m at the base. It was also built directly onto the soft natural subsoil. Small finds included green bottle-glass and burnt mortar from (640).

<h2 style="text-align:center">Trench 11</h2>

A 2.5x2.5m trench was located across the line of a feature shown on the 1st Edition OS map. This trench quickly established that the soft, natural subsoil lay very near to the surface and no evidence of a dyke was found. This would suggest that either no dyke was ever built there or that all traces of it have been completely removed. Again, it was noted that the organic soil in this area is very shallow compared to the rich garden soil within the 'Bede House' enclosure area. Small finds consisted of a metal button (to be confirmed but, possibly, relating to the Royal Scots Fusiliers) from (648).

<h2 style="text-align:center">Trench 4</h2>

Two test pits - 9 and 10 - were extended along dyke [R] from [E] to form Trench 4. This part of the enclosure is located to the south side of the pathway [Y] leading to the building's front door and was noticeably in better preservation than its northern counterpart. These dykes were also constructed of field clearance stones and proved to have been built directly onto the soft natural subsoil and covered by a dark brown, garden soil build-up. Only the lowest course, or footing stones, now survive on the east-facing side of the dyke with the hearting stones now exposed and disturbed. Also evident from this side are the large, inner, west-facing footing

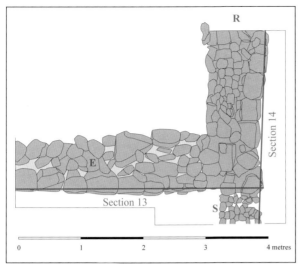

Figure 9. Plan of dykes [E], [R] and [S] to the south of pathway [Y].

stones at two stones high that appear to demonstrate that this was intended as a dyke rather than just a revetment bank. As is the case with the other enclosure dykes, the original height of this dyke remains unknown. A small feature [S] was encountered on the outer corner of dykes [E] and [R] consisting of a layer of smallish stones. One tentative suggestion for this feature might be that it may have been an edging to the trackway leading up to the site. However, a range of other possibilites could be suggested.

An unusual fragment of blue glass was found within the soil that covered this dyke (603) and is thought to be from a late 17th-century bottle. This would fit nicely with the proposed historical dates for the site (see Miller, this volume). Also recovered from (614) was a slate - smoothed on the upper surface - and having a chamfered edge. Chisel marks were also apparent on its underside. Other small finds included green bottle glass and a pot shard from (614), the blue bottle-glass already noted, green bottle-glass and charcoal from (603).

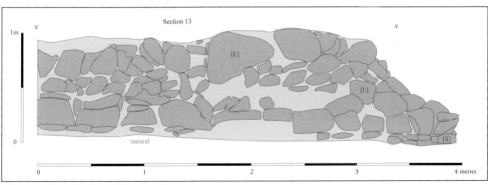

Figure 10. Section 13 (east-facing).

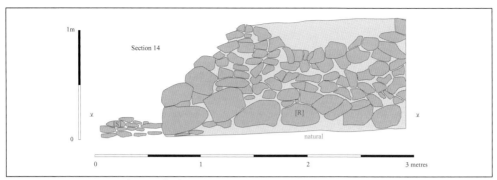

Figure 11. Section 14 (north-facing).

Trench 13

Initially a 1x1m test pit located to the south-facing side of dyke [N] was extended northwards and westwards to form Trench 13. This trench lies opposite Trench 4, across the entrance passage that led to the door of the building.

Trench 13 appears to demonstrate the development, through time, of this section of enclosure dyke(s). It appears to have been altered in accordance with the build-up of garden soils within the enclosure.

The earlier of two features [AK] consists of large outer-facing stones with smaller hearting within that was built directly onto the natural. This feature survives only to one course of stones high and was 0.93m in width. It would appear that this feature formed part of an earlier dyke. It is possible that it formed a low garden wall demarking and retaining garden soil behind. It is clear that a substantial quantity of soil build-up occurred during the occupation of the site and currently survives to a considerable depth of about 0.90m in this corner of the site. It is unlikely that [AK] stood very high and the evidence suggests a possible herbal or grass border lay between it and the entrance path [Y] (see below). This is suggested by a soil-filled space between feature [AK] and the edge of the path (see Photo 5). Figures 12 and 13 show the soil

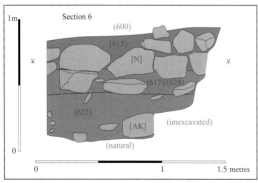

Figure 12. Section 6 (north-facing).
(Also, see Figure 18 below for plan view.)

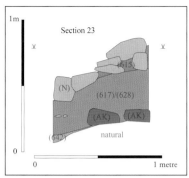

Figure 13. Section 23 (east-facing).

Photo 5. Dyke [N] with [AK] in back right below vertical ranging rod. Note the stones of [N] sitting upon soil build-up between [AK] and the path (below camera).

build-up that occurred after [AK] was built but deposited before [N] was built on top.

The soil accumulation behind [AK] is partly as a result of the area being used as a midden for household waste. It was close to the building's door and would have been a convenient repository for rubbish. This trench proved to be the single most productive area for the recovery of small finds so far excavated. In time, soil had overflowed the first low wall necessitating a replacement. As with feature [AK], [N] was constructed with flattish stone footings on the 'up-slope' and larger stones on the 'lower-slope' with smaller hearting stones between. A considerable quantity of garden soil had overlain feature [AK] before feature [N] was constructed. Most of the small finds found within the soil overburden covering the cobbled path [Y] are thought also to have originated from the garden soil (617) once the upper courses of stone from feature [N] were removed.

The small finds consisted of: green bottle glass, pot shard, slate, clear and frosted glass fragment from (615); prehistoric flint scraper, pot shards, charcoal, green bottle-glass, blue glass bottle fragment (perhaps late 17th century but to be confirmed), slate, animal bone, iron door-hinge eye, clear chimney lamp glass, white glazed tile fragment, possible tile, pipe bowl and stem, iron ?cauldron fragment with rivets from (617). Green bottle-glass, slate, charcoal, pipe bowl and pot shard from (625).

THE EXCAVATIONS OF THE BUILDING

Test Pit 2

A 1x1m test pit was excavated on the outside, north-west corner of the building wall [G]. The wall consisted mainly of large field stones with smaller 'fill-stones' all of which were embedded within an orangey-coloured, sandy-clay material. This material would have presumably made the building draught-proof and would have helped with damp-proofing. This would have been important as the exterior soil-level appears to have been far higher than the internal floor level. This same infill material was found within all the uncovered walls of the building and was much in evidence within the demolition layer that covered the interior of that structure. The wall was built on a protruding footing which had been laid within a cut [AN] through the soft overlaying natural subsoil and onto the hard subsoil below. (See also the evidence from Trench 8 below.) The wall here survived to a height of 0.91m and was 0.80m in width.

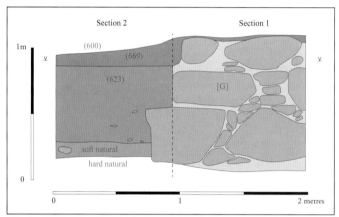

Figure 14. Sections 1 (west-facing) and 2 (south-facing).

A surprising depth of garden loam build-up was noted surrounding this building and clearly suggests that it had been artificially deepened over time, presumably to enrich its fertility for cultivation. This is in stark contrast to the natural soil depth as evidenced by trenches 2, 11 and 14 outside the yard. This strongly suggests that the yard had, for some considerable time, been used for cultivation rather than as a stock enclosure. The small finds consisted of a pot shard handle and a slate fragment from (623).

Test pit 5

A 1x1m test pit was located next to the outer east facing wall [M] of the dwelling. Wall [M] was constructed in the same way as the other walls in this

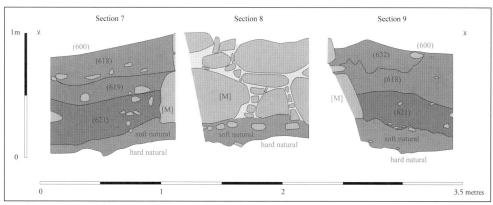

Figure 15. Sections 7 (north-facing), 8 (east-facing) and 9 (south-facing).

structure (see also Test Pit 2 above) but found to be slightly narrower at 0.75m. Wall [M] survived to one course of stones over a footing protruding from the outer side as had wall [G]. Excavation showed that the natural subsoil lay at a depth of 0.64m below the current ground surface which was also the surviving height of the wall. On removing the soft natural subsoil (or possibly re-deposited subsoil) pitting was clearly evident on the hard natural. This was either a glacial weathering surface or pick-axe marks made during preparation of the site for building. The same marks were found in all of the areas excavated down to the hard, natural subsoil within the structure, but not in Test Pit 2. The marks are thought more likely to be evidence of site levelling and their absence from Test Pit 2 suggests the building footprint had been planned prior to the site preparation.

Small finds here included a slate fragment from (618) and slate and charcoal fragments from both (619) and (621).

Trench 15

An initial 2x2m test pit located between dykes [R] and [N] approaching the entrance to the structure was expanded to become the large Trench 15. Figure 16 shows a plan of the cobbled path [Y], garden steps [AI] and the doorway of the building [O].

The cobbled path [Y] was seen to have been constructed directly onto the soft, natural subsoil. Immediately in front of the doorway [O] and built against the southern end of the east wall of the building was found a series of three steps [AI] leading from the pathway [Y] up to the latest garden ground level. Also uncovered was the doorway threshold step that lay at a higher level than the path [Y]. It

Figure 16. Trench 15: entrance path and steps with northern entrance dyke [N].

was also noted that dyke [N] abutted the building wall [M]. To understand the relationship between the contexts within Trenches 13 and 15 dyke [N] was bisected through damaged areas (see Figures 14 and 15 in Trench 13 above).

Small finds in Trench 15 included a pot shard and slate in (627); window glass, green bottle-glass, slate, probable shank of an iron nail, prehistoric flint scraper, pot shard, charcoal and an iron head from a claw hammer from (628). The claw hammer head was found within the soil overlaying the cobbled path [Y]. This was either used during the occupation of the building or during its demolition. The latter seems more likely. Also, pot shards, mortar/plaster, clear glass (shaped and possibly from a chimney lamp) and green bottle-glass from (641). Green bottle-glass and charcoal came from (642) whilst charcoal was found in (643).

Trench 3

An initial 1x2m test pit located inside the building's doorway [O] was extended to form Trench 3. Figure 17 shows the plan of the internal stair masonry [AJ] that faced the entranceway [O].

The south door jamb was found to have a drilled, horizontal hole. This is presumed to have been for either a door hinge or a dowel for a wooden door frame. Two further door jambs were found inside the entrance 'vestibule.' These showed the location of the doorways leading into the north and south gable end rooms respectively. None of these three door jambs had opposite counterparts. This would suggest that only the weight-bearing side were of dressed masonry with the other possibly constructed of timber set against rubble construction. However,

Photo 6. South internal doorway with door jamb stone on right, window sill with drilled recesses for bars in foreground and threshold stone above ranging rod. At the left side of the threshold can be seen a carved recess, probably associated with wooden door frame furniture.

Figure 17. Trench 3: Doorway [O] and probable stair support [AJ].

a carved recess (visible in Photo 6) may be indicative of a setting for a timber fitting, possibly to be associated with a door frame construction. But, it should also be noted that this position coincides with the start of the presumed stairs (see below). Timber supports might also be expected here in order to carry the

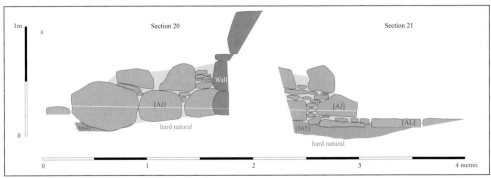

Figure 18. Sections 20 (north-facing) and 21 (south-facing).

Photo 7. Door jamb showing attached metalwork and carved recess for door.

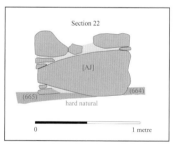

Figure 19. Section 22 (east-facing).

half-floor above the entry vestibule. A further drilled horizontal hole was also found on the north internal door jamb and all three jamb stones had well-executed grooves cut in order to make a snug fit for the doors.

On the top of the southern inner door jamb stone was a dovetailed recess with rusted metal found still to be *in situ*. Part of a metal eye-pivot hinge was recovered from the midden area (Trench 13) located near to the entrance to the dwelling in context (617). This fitted precisely into the recess on the stone (see Photos 6 and 7). If this was the method used for hanging the door, the drilled holes would seem more likely to have been used for mounting a wooden door frame to act as a draught excluder for the closed door to sit against.

A large threshold stone formed a step up into this building with a cobbled floor inside. A worked block of stone was recovered from near this area measuring approximately 0.42m x 0.25m x 0.15m. This had three square/diamond, cut holes evidently for the insertion of window bars (Photo 6). The stone also had a recess on either side - one deeper than the other. These are likely to have been for a window frame or a shutter. This stone block is thought likely to belong to the south gable-end room, though window glass fragments were recovered from both gable ends.

The remains of a masonry structure [AJ] with a width of 0.90m was found in front of the back wall of the vestibule room and is thought to have helped form internal stairs to an upper floor. The stone feature [AJ] rested on the hard natural subsoil on its north side but on soft natural or re-deposited natural subsoil (665) on its south side. This indicates that a slope existed to the underlying hard natural strata (which may be respecting the natural incline of the hill) and that the site was not levelled to true over the entire footprint of the building. Presumably the re-deposited soft natural would have compensated for this slope and helped to form a level base for the masonry structure. Small finds from here included a pot shard from (633), charcoal, green bottle-glass and a pot shard from (634).

Trench 6

Trench 6 was located in the south-east corner of the south gable end of the building. Soil over-burden was removed to reveal a substantial wall [F] of 0.90m in width. Excavation extended along and down this wall on its inner, north side. A substantial amount of demolition material was encountered. The wall survived to four courses of stone with a height of approximately 0.90m. Amongst the demolition layer (611) and the layer above (604), roofing slate fragments were found including one piece with a nail hole. This may indicate the type of roof that this building might once have had. Against the south wall [F], a raised 'platform' feature [T] was uncovered. The east end of this feature lay approximately in the centre of the wall and extended westwards towards the corner of the building's back wall. This 'platform' was found to consist of large stones with smaller pinning stones and had a width of 0.80m and height of approximately 0.45m. The currently-excavated length of this feature is approximately 1.70m but it could not be completely uncovered owing to a standing tree in south-west corner of

Figure 20. South-east corner of building.

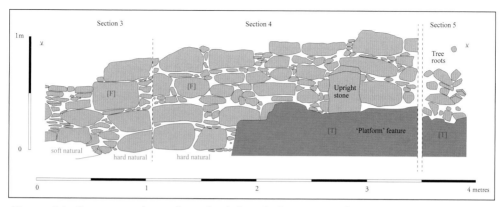

Figure 21. Sections 3 (west-facing), 4 (north-facing) and 5 (east-facing). Section 5 shows surviving demolition rubble covering the western part of the trench.

the building. A lump of peat was found between the stones that formed the top of feature [T] (see Figure 20) but was considered most likely to belong to a later phase and associated with hearth [AC] positioned in front of [T]. Several further peat layers were found on the floor east of feature [T]. It is believed that peat was stacked in this area and used as fuel for hearth [AC]. This hearth may have been created by the workmen during the demolition of the building rather than during the occupation phase. Also recovered from this area were fragments of mortar or plaster, burnt blackened stone and possibly a fire ash-pan fragment. This adds support to the notion that a hearth may have been located in this part of the building (see discussion below). Several iron fragments were also recovered that may have come from kitchen utensils - though this is highly speculative.

Wall [F] was found to be constructed directly onto the hard natural. There were possible pick-axe marks found here as suggested for Test Pit 5 and Trench 8, though not in Test Pit 2 - all indicative of site-levelling only across the footprint of the building. A good stratigraphic sequence was obtained from this area, revealing episodes from building inception through to its dismantling. This can be summarised as follows:

[AN]:   Cut made by site levelling and preparation;
(651):   Orange layer of re-deposited soft natural to infill pick-axe hollows
               formed during site preparation;
(653):   Lower peat layer - approximately 0.01m in depth - is thought to
               originate from a hearth used during the construction of this
               building but before the floor level was raised to its final height;

(647)/(620):   Approximately 0.10m of orangey re-deposited soft natural
                forming a possible floor surface or bedding for a dismantled
                cobbled floor;

(650):   Thin demolition layer containing copious slate fragments. One
                larger fragment next to feature [T] had an iron object adhering
                to its underside. This iron fragment is tubular in shape and may
                be a pan handle fragment. It would appear that the building
                was in the process of being demolished with roofing slate
                fragments laying on the surface before the peat layer (649) was
                deposited on top. Alternatively slate working/trimming might
                have taken place within this room during its occupation.

(649):   Upper peat layer approximately 0. 03m in depth with slate
                fragments found immediately beneath on the interface with
                (650).

Small finds in Trench 6 consisted of: a large animal bone, 1257gms of slate (including one piece with hole), mortar/plaster, green bottle-glass from (604); 4569 gms of slate (including another piece with hole), green bottle-glass, iron object, peat, iron pan handle fragment from (611); peat lump from (649); 579 gms of slate (one piece with tubular iron object [pan handle?]) from (650); slate fragments from (647); peat from (653); pot shard, pipe bowl and stem and more peat from (662). In all 4.2 kgs of roofing slate fragments, seemingly of local provenance, were recovered from Trench 6. Most fragments were left on site.

Trench 7

Trench 7 was located towards the south-west end of the back wall [H] of the building and separated from Trench 6 by a standing tree. As with all the walls

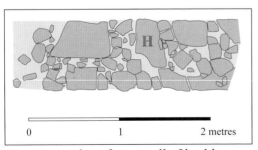

0   1   2 metres

Figure 22. Plan of west wall of building.

of this building, wall [H] had much demolition material filling the interior from the extant wall height down to the interior floor level. Wall [H] was found to be 0.74m in width with a surviving height of approximately 1m. The extant wall stands to two stone courses high on the east-facing side and appears to be up to three stone

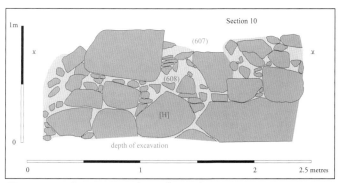

Figure 23. Section 10 (east-facing).

Photo 8. Back wall [H] of building.

courses high on its west-facing side (see Photo 8). The lowest stones of the wall lay directly onto the hard, natural subsoil with re-deposited soft natural subsoil abutting the wall. No cobbled flooring was found in this part of the room.

Small finds from here included window glass, slate and mortar/plaster from (607); slate, chimney-lamp glass, green bottle-glass and pot shards from (608).

Trench 8

Trench 8 was located along the north-west corner of the north gable-end of the building. Wall demolition material filled the interior to the height of walls [G] and [J] down to floor level. Amongst this demolition material was found plaster/mortar and window glass. It would seem that the north and south gable-end rooms were very similar in size and layout with each possessing a window - probably along the east side. Wall [G] was found to be 0.79m in width with an extant height of 0.80m. Wall [J] was found to be 0.87m in width with a surviving height of 0.60m at the west end of the wall and 0.45m at the east. However, this final measurement was only the height from the possible cobbled floor - here left *in situ*. Externally, Test Pit 5 showed the surviving height to have been 0.74m.

On the floor of this room was found hearth [K] lying on top of the floor cobbles and containing burnt material (see Photo 9). Plaster/mortar fragments had fallen on top of this hearth. Also noted were ephemeral traces of a possible

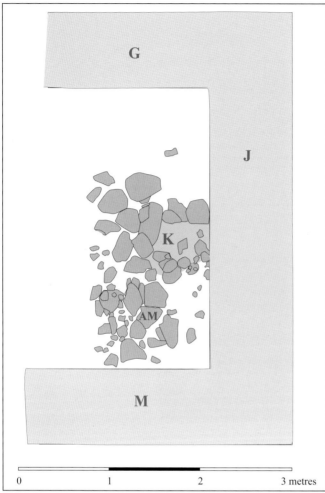

Figure 24. North gable-end of building.

soot outline on the face of wall [J](see Photo 10). This may be indicative of the position of an original hearth. It is considered that feature [K] may be late in date and was a simple hearth used during the demolition of the building by the workmen employed. This is also suggested for the southern end of the building (see above). The surviving cobbles of [K], along with possible associated stones lying to the east, were left *in situ*. Further excavation was only continued in the north-west corner which contained no surviving cobbling.

Walls [G] and [J] were constructed directly onto the hard, natural which was lower on this side of the wall than was found to be the case on the other side in Test Pit 2. As noted above, this indicates that the site had been levelled prior to the construction of the building. Further probable pick-axe marks were evident on the hard, natural surface which was later given a covering of re-deposited natural in order to provide a flat, finished surface. Peculiar to wall [G] is an internal, protruding foundation stone. Although wall footings were observed on the external sides of the building's walls, an internal protruding stone is, so far, unique on this site.

Amongst the small finds recovered was a metal top from a possible perfume bottle with a protruding dispenser tube, along with window glass, mortar/plaster

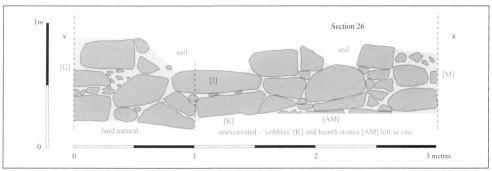

Figure 25. Section 26 (south-facing).

Photo 9. Hearth setting with worked stone at bottom left by root.

Photo 10. Possible black soot marks on wall stones behind hearth stones.

and slate from (605); mortar/plaster from (606); window glass, green bottle-glass from (609) and mortar/plaster from (613).

Also of interest was the recovery of three, worked stone fragments. One of the fragments was recovered from around the hearth [K] (see Photo 9) but is thought likely to have originated elsewhere. It may also be worth noting that a fourth similar fragment was found amongst the stones of dyke [D] in Trench 14. The pieces appear reminiscent of parts of a water trough, though this is speculative.

Small Finds

Very few domestic finds came from the main area of excavation - the building. This may reflect a well-ordered end to the site's usage. As noted above, the removal of structural remains appears to have been carried out tidily and comprehensively. The lack of small finds may indicate that the building did not go through a phased process of abandonment that would have seen the gradual accumulation of debris. It may well be that when the estate decided to stop the charitable funding of the house, it was rapidly removed in order to prevent unwanted squatting or simply to landscape the area in accordance with a new management régime.

Further excavation of the garden area might produce a greater number of finds relating to the period of occupation. It was common practice, until relatively recently, to dispose of household waste in a 'midden' located convenient to a door and thence, periodically, to the garden as compost. Only one likely midden location was encountered at the Bede House site although others may have existed. This midden area was conveniently located near the front door of the building to the north side of the path and within soil context (617). This context provided us with the bulk of our diagnostic small finds: primarily pottery shards and glass. All of the shards recovered would appear to be in keeping with the suggested date range of between the 17 and late 18th centuries.

The following is a brief description of the finds most appropriate to the discussion concerning the period of site usage. A complete catalogue of the small finds, including photographs, is available from the Bailies of Bennachie website. (Editor's note: Please credit any use of the images to Iain Ralston.)

Pottery

As noted above context 617 was particularly rich in pottery shards with 44 being recovered from here and was a far higher concentration than from anywhere else on the site. It is generally regarded that Scottish pre-modern pottery dating is still in its infancy (see Haggarty, Hall & Jones, 2011) and is further complicated by fabrics and styles having been consistent for a long periods of time and, therefore, difficult to date with any precision. However, Photos 11 and 12 show a sherd (small find number 26; catalogue number 130) of what appears to be Scottish Post-Medieval Oxidised Ware (PMOW). The final form as indicated by the sherd is shown in Figure 26 though, as most of the pieces are missing, it is not known whether or not it was a jug - though this is likely. These wares became most common between the late 16th and middle of the 18th century (Haggarty, 2017, 16). (I am

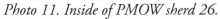

Photo 11. Inside of PMOW sherd 26.

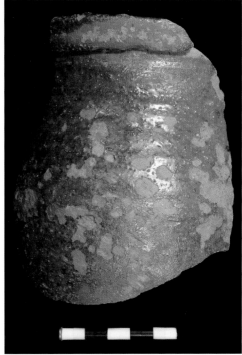

Photo 12. Outside of PMOW sherd 26.

indebted to Gordon Noble for help in identifying this fabric). This particular sherd was sealed beneath dyke [N] and would appear to date to early on in the site's historically-attested occupation.

Glass Vessels (Grateful thanks to Penny Dransart for providing the following consideration of the fragments of bottle glass.)

Two pieces of blue glass appear to date between the late 17th and the mid- to late-18th century. Finds number 17 and

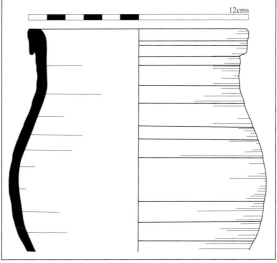

figure 26. Form of PMOW pot as evidenced by the sherd 26.

finds number 29. They may have been used during the lifetime of the structure. However, Murdoch (2008, 54) says these wine bottles were used for ale and beer as well as wine. Liquids were decanted into them and they may have been kept in use for a long time. This limits their potential for dating purposes.

The two green base fragments of wine bottles (finds numbers 33 and 84) with part sidewall are similar to the base of a bottle from Fetternear (small find no. A4685). There are four chronological groups in Murdoch's Fetternear report, and in dating A4685 to the late 18th or early 19th century, he assigns it to the end of his Group 3. The Bennachie bottle base fragments are different sizes, both slightly larger than the Fetternear one and are of a similar glossy green. The two Bennachie bases have significant wear on the base ring and may, therefore, have been re-used.

Window Glass

Approximately 31gms of what is proposed to be window glass was recovered from within the building. It is thought likely that a small window existed at each gable end room.

Metalwork

Metalwork would seem to include domestic items, structural elements, such as door hinge fragments and nails and the the head of a claw hammer. The latter may have been residual from the demolition process.

Slate

Approximately 6,846gms of slate was recovered from the south gable room in Trenches 6 (contexts 604, 611, 615, 650) and 7 (contexts 607, 608). This relatively large quantity contrasts with only 274gms of slate being recovered from context (605) in Trench 8 from the north gable end room and none at all from the central 'vestibule'. This may indicate that the southern area was used in the processing or stacking of slates during the demolition of the building. Alternatively, the roof may have already partly collapsed prior to demolition. But, it must also be noted that there is evidence that some of this material may have come from slate working within the building during its occupation or construction.

The recovery of a further 1,231gms of slate material from the proposed midden area in context 617 may indicate that slate working had taken place within the building during its occupation with the waste material being deposited along with the rest of the household's rubbish. However, the late dating of glass bottle fragments noted above may indicate that the midden area was still being used up to the turn of the end of the 18th century. This would accord with Miller's analysis (this volume) of the building's timeline.

Flint (Grateful thanks to Angela Groat for providing the following descriptions of the flints.)

Small Find No 25, Context 617.
Small primary flake of dark to light brown with cream cortex. No signs of retouch. 22mm long by 19mm wide.

Small Find No 7, Context 617.
Inner flake of brown flint. No signs of retouch, 29mm long by 17mm wide.

Small Find No 11, Context 628.
Secondary flake of grey flint with remains of cream cortex. 35mm long x 17mm wide.

It is thought likely that the three flint finds might be residue from a much earlier site phase or more likely have been imported onto the site with loam soil gathered from elsewhere and deposited to build up the garden area. It should be noted that Bronze or Iron Age hut circles are known in the near vicinity.

Discussion

Covering the entire site was a naturally-generated, build-up of organic soil created by the decay of forest litter, i.e. pine needles and other herbaceous debris. Below this covering was found either relict soil from the yard or demolition debris from the dismantling of the building and some of the dykes: orangey, clay-bonding from the building walls and displaced stones from the dykes.

The excavations have shown that the building was 12.58m long by 4.46m wide along the external, north gable wall and approximately 4.50m along the external south gable wall. Internally, the ground floor consisted of a room at either end with an entrance 'vestibule' and staircase between. The two rooms appear each to have had windows - possibly with glass - and one, at least, appears to have had window bars. The survival of slates with nail holes along with many other

Photo 11. Trench 6 at the south end of the building. In the corner can be seen the original floor level and, next to the ranging rod, a small baulk showing the occupation layers topped by a peat deposit. This peat store is considered to have been associated with the secondary hearth stones seen bottom right. Behind these stones is a platform that may have been the site of an earlier hearth.

fragments, suggests the building had a slate roof. All slate may well have been sourced locally. The vestibule was cobbled and some parts or all of the two rooms may also have been similarly floored. (Though there is more evidence to suggest this to have been the case in the northern room.)

The main entrance door opened inwards as did the two inner doors from the central vestibule. The doors seem to have been hung on iron eyes hinges that were embedded in the masonry of the door jambs. A wooden frame may have been fitted by using the horizontally-drilled holes. This would have sealed the door against draughts when shut. The fit would have been made particularly snug by a neatly-cut groove carved into the stone jamb. Similar carpentry appears to be demonstrated by the stone with window bar holes that also had grooves carved for the fitting of either a frame, shutters or both.

The well-built, stone platform at the rear of the 'vestibule' suggests the existence of internal stairs giving access to an upper storey. It is hard to believe that the platform was simply a support for wooden stairs. It is more likely that steps were built upon the platform but that these were robbed. This would have created a stepped structure more commonly found situated externally on buildings of this period that gave access to an upper storey. This 'internalisation' of such a structure suggests an interesting architectural development.

The excavations have also indicated probable building techniques employed, at least for the surface and floor preparations (see Photo 11). Firstly, the site was stripped of organic soil and approximately 0.20m depth of soft, natural subsoil was shovelled off for re-use. The hard, natural subsoil was levelled to the required building footprint, probably, by pick-axe, resulting in a pitted surface. The wall lines were laid out, the lower courses constructed and the (probably) previously-removed soft natural subsoil was re-introduced to level the pitted surface (651). A thin, peaty layer appears to reflect a short-lived occupation phase (653). This may well have been a simple worker's hearth used during the construction process. However, there was no evidence of building debris mixed in with the peat. The other possibility is that this was a first phase of proper occupation covered over when a new floor was introduced (647/620).

The demolition of the building appears to have been undertaken with care with materials removed, presumably, for use elsewhere. Only fragments of roofing slate survived and most of the useable stones were taken away. The rough hearths at either end of the house appear to be the result of the presence of the demolition squad or other people subsequently seeking a bit of shelter on the hill. Either, whilst working on the hill, as rough shelter for seasonal workers or even as 'picknickers'. The green bottle-glass found within the destruction layers (e.g. 609) may have belonged to any such people.

The lack of 19th-century artefactual remains speaks volumes when contrasted with the evidence from the squatter colony just around the hill (Oliver et al, 2013, 110-111). There, copious amounts were found; here virtually no such evidence was discovered. It cannot be doubted that this structure was out of use by 1800.

There are other interesting details to be seen within specific architectural features associated with the building. The steps [AI] leading from beside the door gave access to the garden area. No other means of gaining access to this area is evident. There was no 'back door' from the dwelling nor any notable sign of a gate along the garden dykes. Further excavation would be required to establish if steps [AI] are laid directly onto the garden soil without foundations or if stone foundations are present. No foundations would indicate that the steps were laid as and when required as the ground level rose and were only ever intended for garden access. Foundation stones may indicate that external stairs may once have existed here to access the upper floor. Whether such stairs complemented or were earlier than the internal stairs would be a moot point. Dalmaik Old Parish Church at Drumoak had two means of accessing the upper floor, albeit both were external in that instance.

The relationships of the entrance path [Y], the garden dykes [N] and [AK] and the building are also interesting and suggest a staged development. It appears that the building was initially laid out with a cobbled path [Y] leading up to its doorway. Part of the original plan, excavation would suggest, included a narrow garden 'border' between the path and the dyke. This is demonstrable for the north side and may be suggested for the opposite side of the pathway as well. The northern border was backed by the retaining dyke [AK] - its basal course being at the same level as [Y].

In time, the garden level rose to a substantial height and this necessitated the building of another retaining dyke [N]. Where this soil came from is an interesting question. Such 'plaggen' soils are known from many sites around Scotland and within the immediate locality at the Colony (Oliver *et al*, 2016, 359). Historically, the Barony Book of Forbes frequently fulminates against the 'casting of divots' from the local meadows and fields - thereby enhancing an individual's soils at the expense of the community's.[1] Usually such soils derive from the stripping of turf from less agriculturally productive ground in the vicinity. In this case, this may well have been from higher up the hill - it being more practical to transport it down from agriculturally less-used land than carry up good soil from the productive fields below.

On the removal of stone from the site during the demolition phase, it is presumed that dyke [N] was reduced, along with the other dykes of the garden enclosure, down to ground level and leaving only the lower courses of stone behind. This gives us a good indication of the quantity of soil present and highlights the contrast between the garden area and the thin soil outwith the enclosure dykes. The dyke between [N] and the north-east corner was completely removed and only the soil lynchet indicates its former position. Interestingly, this was not in line with its opposite number between the entrance-way and the south-east corner of the yard.

---

1   For example, page 254 in the Barony Book for 1664 [Scottish History Society, 1919]: "... ordaines the haill tenentis according to formall act maid yairanent who cast faill or deffiotes eithe rwith foot spades of flatteres spades in meadow or lone or in hening, they sall pey..."

It is also worth noting at this point that this discrepancy is not apparent from the Ordnance Survey drawing as also is the fact that the building does not sit squarely within its enclosure as shown on that plan. The latter point may add credibility to the notion that the building and yard are not contemporary. The suggestion that the dykes were preceded by an earlier earthen bank may be important to this line of reasoning.

The garden dyke [N] could be seen to simply abut the building rather than being bonded into its stonework. This is not surprising as it has just been noted that [N] was a replacement dyke for [AK]. Unfortunately, the relationship of [AK] could not be seen owing to the roots of a mature standing tree.

More problematic are slithers of evidence that merely hint at further architectural details. For instance, fairly substantial amounts of plaster were found in particular situations within the building: at either end and, especially, around the main doorway. The latter may be the result of the passage of the demolition team in and out of the building or it may be related to the door structure itself. The concentration in the north room appeared to be at the end where any hearth might be expected. Earlier suggestions concerning the necessity for a 'hanging-lum' may be relevant to this concentration. (Clearly, a two-storey structure would need to have some venting mechanism if there was a fire on the ground floor.)

Internal and external ground levels around the building are also puzzling. It has been noted above that the extant height of the back wall survived to approximately 1m high internally and this was after the removal of the stone to the contemporary garden surface. Clearly, the ground floor, at the end of its period of use, was a metre below ground level. This would have resulted in a serious damp problem. But, as Section 23 shows (page 117), the top of the surviving dyke [N] was a good 0.50m higher than the surviving stones of the earlier wall [AK]. It is not impossible that, in its earliest from, the ground floor may have been much closer in level to the outside ground level. Any difference may have been mitigated by keeping the immediate area around the house free of topsoil - in fact, providing a walkway around. Such an arrangement would bring it into line with the later Colony structures. Shepherds Lodge can be shown to have had a pathway separating the house from its garden (Foster, B., this volume) and Burnside still has a gulley behind the house to help prevent penetrating damp. If this was the case, the question begins to centre on why the landscaping changes occurred. Why was there a decision to try to increase the productive capacity of the ground and why was the comfort of the inhabitants sacrificed to those ends? Or, did that increase of soil occur after the desertion of the house during a period when the rich garden soil was still being used by an absentee gardener. The finds relating to the very end of the 18th century may suggest such a possibility

Finally, there are still questions relating to the enclosure dykes to be answered. What is the meaning of the strange 'dog-leg' noted in Trench 9? And why were the dykes north and south of the entrance-way so offset? The structure as a unit - dykes and building - will have formed an impressive statement in the landscape as viewed from below across a fairly wide area. Was there a design element to this 'off-setting' that, at present, evades us? As ever, many questions have been answered, but many new questions have consequentially arisen. But, that's just archaeology, I suppose!

CONCLUSION

The low, earthen lumps hid a surprising depth of well-built, stone walling that supplied good evidence for the construction and architecture of the building. More than enough survived to permit an assessment of the remains and to compare them to the few but telling descriptions and dates provided by the documentary sources (see Miller, this volume). It is hard not to be drawn to the conclusion that this extremely well-constructed, slate-roofed, two-storeyed building with window bars was built by the Erskines on their estate. The artefactual evidence suggests it was built in the 17th century and was out of use by the end of the 18th. Its siting adjacent to 'Beid House Park' suggests an association with a charitable function. In all, it is difficult not to be persuaded that this is, in fact, the 'hospital' built by the Erskines in or around 1639 and that its later association with a notion of it being a 'Bede House' developed from that initial foundation.

FURTHER SITE DATA

Further data is available in digital format from the Bailies' website. Please feel free to download it from there. The additional files are:

1.   XL spreadsheet containing further information about individual contexts.
2.   Word file containing a full list of small finds and their contexts.

ACKNOWLEDGEMENTS

Many thanks to the Bailies of Bennachie for sponsoring the project and to Jackie Cumberbirch for her personal support. To Finlay Morrison, Estate Manager of the Pittodrie Estate and to Macdonald Hotels for permission to work on the land. A special thanks are due to Barry Foster for proposing this project to the Bailies of Bennachie and a sincere thank you to all the Bailies of Bennachie that helped with the fieldwork. Of those Colin Miller must receive a special mention for organising and carrying-out the brashing of spiky branches on site prior to work beginning for the purposes of creating safe working conditions for diggers and visitors. Penny Dransart very kindly imparted many words of wisdom regarding the small finds as well as offering much insightful knowledge concerning the wider historical landscape. Also I wish to offer my sincere gratitude to all the volunteers that participated in the digging; without them this project could not have succeeded. In no particular order: Brian Cornock, Colin Miller, Andrew Wainwright, David Irving, Barry Foster, David Peter, Irvine Ross, David Richards, Steven Cromar, Alistair Stenhouse, Ann Baillie, Charlotte Baillie, Allan Will, Richard Gordon, Max Williams, Jamie Falconer and Peter Thorn. I also wish to add a special thank you to Nadine, my daughter and a junior Bailie. Her keen eye-sight and reasoning abilities were helpful and impressive in pre-excavation stages. Nadine noted many features that otherwise might have been overlooked and came up with many viable interpretations of those features.

THE SOCIAL AND LANDSCAPE CONTEXT OF THE PITTODRIE HOSPITAL

Colin Shepherd

There are two things wrong with the title noted above. Firstly, when the hospital was commissioned by the Erskines in 1639 (see Miller, this volume), the estate was known as the barony of Balhalgardy rather than Pittodrie. Secondly, by the time Pittodrie became the recognised address for the 'Bede House' the word hospital had ceased to be used. So, to be correct, we should either refer to the Balhalgardy Hospital or the Pittodrie Bede House. Whether there was ever a relationship between the two or whether the site of either can be recognised were aims of this project.[1]

What we know is that a building on a shoulder of Bennachie on the Pittodrie Estate has now been partially excavated. It appears to have been two storeys in height. The documentary evidence suggests that the Balhalgardy hospital was also of two storeys (*ibid.*). A sentence in the 'View of the Diocese of Aberdeen' (*ibid.*; Collections for a History of the Shires of Aberdeen and Banff, 1843, 657-658) written in the early 18th century says it was three units in width. This also suits the excavated remains. But, that is where the descriptive evidence stops. We do know, however, that the artefactual evidence from the excavation suggests the structure to have been in use between the late 17th and the end of the 18th centuries. This would also fit with our account of its date of foundation and McConnochie makes it clear that the Bede House had fallen out of use a long time before he wrote and survived only as footings and folk memory (1890, 27). The construction of the excavated building itself is certainly in keeping with the quality anticipated of a substantial landowner aiming to impress.

One major objection may be that the hospital was said to have lain in the Chapel of Garioch, whilst the excavated remains sit just over the parish boundary in Oyne. However, as the hospital was built from the revenues of holdings historically belonging to the Chapel of Garioch (Act of Scottish Parliament 17/11/1641), this might be considered sufficient reason for it to have been thought of as comprising part of the Chapel of Garioch[2]. Countless examples of portions of one parish

1   *A more complete analysis of the documentary background to this project is supplied by Colin H. Miller elsewhere in this volume.*

2   *That the estate was named Balhalgardy rather than Pittodrie should cause no surprise: a rental of 1771 (MS2392) shows that the former comprised 6 ploughlands compared with Pittodrie's 2. That this was also the case over a hundred years earlier can be shown by a rental for 1636 (MS3043/70).*

sitting isolated within an adjoining parish survive across Britain. Examples in the North-east include Philorth (Fraserburgh), Aberdour and Methlick. This example, therefore, should not occasion too much surprise[3]. Also, as the endowment was of a personal nature, it is likely that the recipients were residents of the estate rather than the parish - the two not being coterminous.

The terminology used for the building - hospital - raises questions. In medieval usage, such a term can fulfil a variety of outcomes. Within a post-medieval, post-Reformation world the use of the term becomes increasingly worrisome. Cowan and Easson (1976) have compiled, to date, the most complete record of pre-Reformation religious establishments in Scotland. Canmore, the HES database, can be used to supply further post-Reformation examples that have an extant archaeological or architectural record. By utilising both, the following figures are derived:

Pre-Reformation hospital foundations	144
Post-Reformation hospital foundations	12
Pre-Reformation uses of the term 'bede'	7
Post-Reformation uses of the word 'bede'	21
Pre-reformation use of word 'poor' in foundation charter	48
Use of words 'sick', 'infirm' or 'leper' in foundation charter	25
Use of words 'traveller'/'pilgrim'/'guest' in foundation charter	7
Use of word 'alms' in foundation charter	37
Number of charitable institutions that survived till 17th c.	33
Number of pre Reformation institutions defunct by mid 16th c.	37
'Guesstimated' number of institutions that fell foul of the Reformation (144 − [33 + 37] = 74)	74
Approx. number extant at time of Reformation (144 − 37)	107
Approx. number in existence post Reformation (12 + 33)	45

(These figures may not be entirely correct owing to the inability of this writer to access all of the original charters. Great emphasis has been placed here upon Cowan and Easson's faithful reproduction of precise terminology. However, the balance of the figures is unlikely to be badly awry and should be suitable for the simple diagnostics suggested here. A further caveat is that we just do not know the foundation dates and destruction dates of many of the institutions. These factors help to account for the discrepancies apparent in the totals noted above.)

---

3   *Even isolated chunks of Banffshire could be found floating adrift in eastern Aberdeenshire into the second half of the 19th century.*

It is worth mentioning that place-names can be used to indicate former hospital sites but, as with all place-name evidence, need to be treated with care. Not too far away, between Inverurie and Whiterashes, is a small farm named 'spital'. Although, in many instances, this place-name does indicate former hospital sites, it can also simply refer to land that was gifted to a hospital situated elsewhere in order to generate income for its needs. This is the most likely explanation in this instance. Spitalmyre in Banff, however, does accurately note a post-Reformation foundation for 8 poor women whilst Spitalhill in Aberdeen marks the area of the medieval leper house in Aberdeen.

What may be noted regarding the figures quoted above is how many foundations for the poor, sick and needy were created before the Reformation and how many were created afterwards. Work by Penny-Mason & Gowland (2014, 162-194) in their study of skeletal disease in cemeteries from across Britain has drawn attention to the high mortality occasioned by the Reformation and how long it took for the removal of the social service supplied by the Catholic church to be replaced by the new regime. The thrust of Scottish laws regarding the poor was, from a statute of James I in 1424 onwards, primarily an attempt to limit the numbers of wandering 'vagabonds' and 'idle men'. The laws were designed to segregate the 'needy poor' from these 'vagabonds'. In 1503 the 'aged and the infirm' were to be aided by collections within their own parishes and were permitted to beg only within those limits. Enshrined within the laws was the concept that all who could, should work and, laudable as this may sound, the methods employed - whipping, though stopping short of torture - sound a tad extreme to modern ears. During the course of the 16th and 17th centuries, the legal provisions became increasingly harsh (Nicholls, 1856, 7; see Appendix for further detail).

A further consideration may be the popularity of Sir Walter Scott's writings during the course of the 19th century and the influence his works had on the use and understanding of the term 'bede'. This is particularly pertinent to the notion of the 'blue gowners' as noted in 'The Antiquary'. Another is the package of 'Enlightenment' values associated with Adam Smith, Malthus and even our own home-grown Archibald Grant in which poverty was equated with poor character (Shepherd, 2015, 64-67). A 'bedesman' might be considered worthy of alms whilst a 'poor' person/potential 'vagabond' might not. Pre-Reformation foundations abound with words associated with 'giving', though with little evidence of reciprocation being required: 'poor', 48 times; 'alms', 37 times and the various categories of 'sick', 25 times. In other words, 110 out of 144 foundation charters of institutions during the pre-Reformation period recorded charity requiring no repayment. Of the 45 in existence after the Reformation, 21 employed the word 'bede' signifying a '*quid pro quo*' arrangement - even though, in a post-Reformation environment, the notion of helping lairds and their families through purgatory with prayer must have been fairly anachronistic.

In Samuel Johnson's dictionary (1756) a 'beadsman' was defined as 'a man employed in praying for another'. This suggests active employment rather than the receiving of 'alms'.[4] Even within the context of James VI and the now famous 'gowns of blue cloth' claimed by Walter Scott in 'The Antiquary' to be for the 'King's Bedesmen', the wording in the accounts of Sir Robert Melvill, the Treasurer-Deputy of King James VI notes payment to the King's 'Almoner' of money to buy 'twentie four gownis of blue clayth, to be gevin to xxiiij auld men...' This sounds more like a gift of alms. The same can be said of the 'twentie fyve pund sterling, to be gevin to the puir be the way in his Majesteis progress' - this time by the deputy 'Elimozinar' (Almoner) to his majestie. Again, this is a gift of alms with no expectation of *quid pro quo*.

In Edward Phillips' dictionary, first published in 1658, 'hospital' is defined as 'properly an House of Charity founded by the Prince or State, for the Entertainment and Relief of Poor, Sick, Impotent, or Aged Persons: an Alms-house'. His definition of 'bede-house' is: 'an Hospital, or Almes-House for Bedes-Men, or poor People, who pray'd for their Founders and Benfactors'[5]. 'Alms': 'whatever is freely given to the Poor for God's Sake'; 'Alms-House': 'a House built by a Man or Woman in a private Capacity, and endow'd with a sufficient Revenue for the Maintenance of a certain Number of poor, aged, or disabled Persons.' (Phillips, 1720.) These definitions are important as they relate to a time very close to the foundation date of the Pittodrie 'hospital'. The 'hospital' of Pittodrie may be considered to have been founded by the state in as much as it was the state that granted the permission. By 1758, the construction of the Royal Naval Hospital at Stonehouse, Plymouth must have consigned the word's other definitions to the past. This was a place designed to care for the sick and wounded in special 'wards' and laid the blueprint for today's hospitals (Military Hospitals in the United States, 15). Therefore, whilst an older definition of 'hospital' may have persisted till Johnson's dictionary of 1756, within a few short years, such usage had been superseded. This may well explain the change of name for the Pittodrie 'hospital' so that, by the time of the 1771 rental, the 'hospital' had become a 'bede house'.

---

4   *He defines 'hospital' in two ways: '1. a place built for the reception of the sick, or support of the poor. 2. a place for shelter or entertainment.'*

5   *Note the past tense used for 'pray'd' - post-Reformation, such a thing might not have been considered 'politically correct'.*

Why the name chosen was 'bede house' rather than 'alms-house' or 'poor house' may well be wrapped up in sentiments already discussed as present in the Scottish Poor Laws since the 16th century. In brief, 'Bedesmen' could be seen as supplying a service for their payment and, thus, socially acceptable. 'The term 'Alms-house' appears to have almost fallen into disuse, probably because no such thing existed. 'Poor Houses' by this time were, in effect, the forerunner of the later 'workhouses' where all were expected to contribute towards their keep. They may have hinted too much of potential 'vagabonds' in the neighbourhood for 'polite' usage.

Bishop Gavin Dunbar's foundation charter for his hospital at Aberdeen in 1531 makes no mention of the word 'bedesmen' or even of the *quid pro quo* of 'prayer for cash'. But, perhaps more importantly, his notion of Christian charity in the 16th century stands in stark contrast to earlier perceptions. In the words of Gavin Dunbar (translated by Prof. McAleese, 2012, 1, 5), "...when something is left after supplying the needs of the church and our own life, ...give of thy bread to the hungry and the poor..." (*ibid*; REA I, 401-406). During the 13th century, in cases of hunger attended by the lack of money to buy food, theft was not considered, by the Catholic church of Thomas Aquinas, to be a crime since 'nede ne hath no lawe' (Firth Green, 2007, 11). Clearly charity had nose-dived from an obligation to share worldly goods to become an ethic of giving away just some of the surplus. During the next hundred years, the concept of Christian charity was to plummet to an all-time low. Wills from other parts of Britain show a developing apathy towards making bequests for the poor. At the beginning of the 16th century, such bequests appear to be common. By the end of the 16th century such bequests were rare (Dallas and Sherlock, 2002, 93-107).

The situation was not helped by the crown. James I appears to have had a genuine interest in the reform of religious foundations (Cowan & Easson, 1976, 16) and an Act of Parliament (1425/3/3) required them to adhere to their original purposes. This was repeated by James II (1458/3/13) in which Act a list of local persons responsible for visiting the royal foundations in each diocese was noted. For Aberdeen this responsibility fell to Lord Forbes and the Abbot of Deer. But, royal 'reform' increasingly became little more than an excuse to appropriate religious holdings for dispersal amongst royal favourites (Cowan & Easson, 1976, 21-4). By Act of Parliament (A1516/11/2), the hospital of St. Mary the Virgin near Montrose was 'refounded' by James V in favour of the Dominicans as a place where prayers could be said by the clerics for the souls of his family and some of the lands alienated to loyal henchmen. However, in this instance, the hospital was later reconstituted to its former purpose as a place of refuge for the poor by Mary in 1559x60. This particular hospital even managed to survive for a while after the Reformation (Cowan & Easson, 1976, 186).

Regarding the Pittodrie foundation, it may be important that the Erskines were still, during the 17th century, supporters of the Catholic faith, in keeping with many other great families in the North-east at this time. It is certainly not inconceivable that their sentiments were more in tune with pre-Reformation ideals than with any proto-enlightenment notions.

In turning to the landscape siting of the 'hospital', there are a few concerns relating to how the building may have been used. The building is isolated and not apparently close to a water supply. However, lades built during the 19th century for the Pittodrie Estate and subsequent drainage activities may well have removed a former supply. So, this issue remains moot. In the present day, the building is remote and, whilst wooded, appears isolated. This is, in large part, also a product of subsequent landscape management. It sat upon two locally-important routeways. One survived to be included in Robertson's map of 1822 and the other has survived as 'The Turnpike' (see Figure 26). To the south these routeways linked Pittodrie with two crossing points across the River Don, at the Boat of Forbes at Keig and at Fetternear. Both places were also sites of regional power: a major residence of the Forbeses at Keig and the Leslie 'palace' at Fetternear. The two routes - once joined near the hospital - led north and west around the shoulder of Bennachie to where they divided once more to lead west to meet the Mar Road to Kildrummy and north-west via Insch to Huntly and the north. South-east from Pittodrie led the main route back to Aberdeen. In other words, the hospital site sat in the middle of a well-established route network linking 'the great and the good' of the region. From its perch on the shoulder of Bennachie, it would also have glowered over the landscape to the north and east - its doorway viewed through an impressive entrance-way flanked by stone dykes. It was clearly making a statement in the landscape, presumably related to the role of the Erskines in the vicinity. But, its positioning also suggests a pre-occupation with a former attribute of 'hospitals' prior to the mid 18th century - that of providing a place of rest for travellers. A recently excavated 'almshouse' was endowed by James McFarlane at Creag a'Phuirt on Loch Lomond between 1612 and 1625 with the sole purpose of supplying shelter to travellers passing through (James, 2017). The stone sill with holes for window bars discovered at Pittodrie (see below) might suggest a refuge for travellers during the uncertain times of the 17th century rather than exclusively the home of 'poor' folk. Hospitals frequently fulfilled both roles.

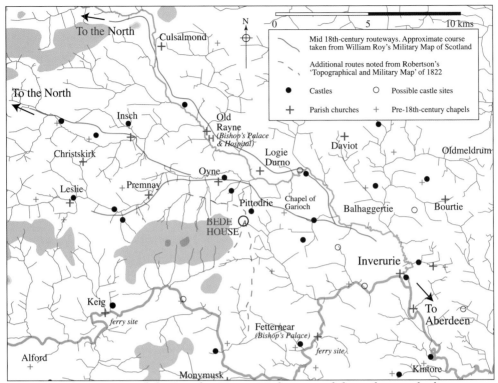

Figure 27. The area around the Pittodrie Estate. Higher ground shown by grey shading.

Consideration of the immediate surroundings of the 'hospital' may also be instructive. Surviving plantation banks still delineate woodlands present in the 18th century. The estate rental of 1771 (MS 2392) lists these plantations. Only one - Beidhouse Park - shows any alteration in size to that defined by the rental. Colin Miller has demonstrated that it was formerly bounded on its east side by the faint remains of a plantation bank but that, during the ensuing years between 1771 and the Ordnance survey of 1866 x 1867, it had grown so that its eastern boundary had become the present 'Turnpike' (pers. comm.). Beid House Park was later to become Bede House Wood. North of Beid House Park lay Farquharson Park and, to the north of that, lay Maiden Castle Park.

These areas of woodland are clearly depicted on the early 19th-century maps of Robertson and Thomson but also appear to be alluded to in Roy's survey of the 1740s - though not in detail. The parks appear to have been constructed with the intent of articulating with the existing routeway passing the Bede House - wide 'loans' being left between Farquharson's Park and Maiden Castle Park. The use of the term 'park' at this time in the North-east is suggestive. By the mid

19th century it was well-established as indicating an enclosed field, usually for grazing. Its medieval usage had been to define an enclosed area pertaining to the lord's resource management. This included (but was not limited to) deer and other animals 'of the chase' as well as timber stocks and areas of woodland pasture. It is the last that suggests how this definition may have changed from medieval to modern usage. By the time of the Ordnance Survey, these areas of timber were recorded as 'woods' rather than 'parks'. However, the earlier name does hint at another possible use for these enclosed areas rather than as simple plantations.

Be that as it may, the excavations appear to show that the 'yard' associated with the Bede House preceded the plantation dykes. So, if the 'hospital' was built - along with its yard dykes - in the 1640s, the plantation dykes would have been built later. But, the excavations also showed that the yard dykes appear to have cut through an earlier earthen linear feature. So, the 'hospital' may have been built within a pre-existing enclosure that pre-dated the mid 17th century. At the moment this is mere speculation and further archaeological work is required to test these possibilites. What does seem certain, however, is that when the hospital was built in the 1640s, it would have been the most prominent feature on this part of the hill with no trees to diminish that prominence.

It is appropriate, finally, to consider the question of how common these hospitals were across the North-east at this time. As noted above, there were very few founded after the Reformation. Charters for a 'hospice and guesthouse' for weary travellers at Old Rayne was granted to Bishop Elphinstone in 1493 and 1498[6] but this does not necessarily mean that it was ever constructed. It was to be for travellers going between Elgin and Aberdeen. There were clearly houses for the poor and infirm at Aberdeen and a hospital for poor men was established by William Forbes at Tarves. Cullen had a couple of foundations and the leper house of Rathven appears, ultmately, to have become a 'bede house'. An undated abstract rental from the estate (GD225/1029) notes the laird's obligation to the poor there as follows:

> 'The heritor pays yearly to 6 Beadmen in the hospital of Rathven 6 bolls of meall @ 8st. and 10/- sterling in money for which no deduction is made in the within rental as the priviledge of presenting these poor men is to be disponed with the estate.'

(It should be noted that obligation is owed by the estate and not the parish. This would seem to be the same situation as at Pittodrie, noted above. At 64 pecks to the boll (https://www.sizes.com/units/boll.htm), the payment at Pittodrie and

---

6   *I'm grateful to Eileen Clare Grant for drawing my attention to this reference.*

Rannes seem fairly similar with the Pittodrie bedesmen receiving 52 pecks of meal and 26 pecks of malt per year. At Rannes, each had 64 pecks of meal but 10/- in cash instead of the 26 pecks of malt - presumably to be converted to liquid malt at the local inn!).

It is, therefore, interesting to note that the North-east appears to have contained a relatively large proportion of the post-Reformation hospitals in Scotland and it is probably not inappropriate to see this as being the result of pre-Reformation religious tendencies in the area. If Aberdeen maintained at least three of them well into the post-Reformation period, the total for the North-east would be in the order of 10 out of the national figure of around 45. (Though this is based upon the, admittedly, incomplete and estimated numbers noted above.)

The Balhalgardy hospital appears to be one of the last examples in Scotland of a charitable foundation that has its roots in a pre-Reformation religious mindset. It appears to reflect an attitude of personal piety and obligation to the community in a period before such care became seen as a secular responsibility. Its apparent name change to the 'Bede House' may reflect the period of social ambivalence and exclusion that we now term 'the Enlightenment'. That it failed to survive this callous interlude is, perhaps, not surprising.

Appendix[1]
(taken from Nicholls, 1856)

Under a statute of 1579 Parish inhabitants were to be taxed to the level required to sustain their own poor. However, if the appointed parish overseers considered any of the poor capable of work, they were forced to undertake it. From 1592 the kirk sessions became sole arbiters of the law for relief (32), though by 1662 the responsibility had been passed to justices to appoint overseers. This new act permitted manufacturing companies to seize 'vagabonds' and to set them to work for no wages. Moreover, the companies would be paid by the parish of domicile of the 'vagabond' for each day's labour for the next 3 years (64). They then had to work for a further seven years for the company for their meat and clothing. (Though this Act appears to have been short-lived if operational at all, it does give the measure of the general mindset regarding poverty at the time.) In 1672 came the 'correction houses' in which the 'indigent poor' were to be housed and set to work[2]. Genuinely ill people were to be housed at the parish's expense but, if not enough funds could be found, they were given a badge and permitted to beg around their own parish. Poor children were given to those who wanted them for work and would have to stay with them and work for 'meat and clothes' till 30 years of age (69). Authority for overseeing this was placed back in the hands of the kirk. Few burghs appear to have built such houses, however, and a further Act of 1698 re-inforced the call for them (83). It has been noted that the lines demarcating 'deserving poor' from 'vagabonds' was forever in a state of flux (89). Nicholls quotes Alison's 'Remarks on the Poor Laws of Scotland,' (1844, 8):

> "They grant to the poor in almost all parts of the country an allowance utterly inadequate to their maintenance, knowing perfectly that the only means by which this deficiency can be supplied is common begging; and then they punish as criminals, persons who have been reduced to this degradation by their own maladministration of the laws designed for the protection of those very persons." (108)

---

1   *It is to be noted that this report was written in 1856 - not normally a time renowned for its soft, socialist views.*

2   *Overseers were permitted to whip them but had to stop short of torture (70).*

SOURCES

Act of Scottish Parliament 17/11/1641, Edinburgh, 17 November 1641, Act regarding the erection of the hospital of Balhalgardy.

Act of Scottish Parliament, 12/03/1425, Perth, Concerning 'Hospitals' (*hostillaris*), 1425/3/3.

Act of Scottish Parliament, 06/03/1458, Edinburgh, The Reform of Hospitals, 1458/3/13.

Act of Scottish Parliament, 13/11/1516, Edinburgh, Legislation: Private Acts, A1516/11/2.

Collections for a History of the Shires of Aberdeen and Banff, Spalding Club, A View of the Diocese of Aberdeen (MDCCXXXII), 67-658.

Samuel Johnson's Dictionary of the English Language, 1756, online edition.

MS 3043/70, 1636, Rental of Logie Durno parish, Aberdeen University Special Collections.

MS 2392, 1771, Rental Book of the Pittodrie Estate, Aberdeen University Special Collections.

GD 225/1029, undated abstract rental of Rannes lands, National Records of Scotland.

William Roy's Military Map of Scotland, 1747-1755.

Topographical and Military map of the Counties of Aberdeen, Banff and Kincardine, 1822.

John Thomson's Atlas of Scotland, 1832.

1st edition Ordnance Survey 6" and 25" to the mile, 1866 x 1867.

Military Hospitals in the United States, Volume V, undated, http://history. amedd.army.mil/booksdocs/wwi/MilitaryHospitalsintheUS/introduction.htm, 14-27.

The Macaulay Institute for Soil Research, Soil Survey of Scotland, 1984

Barony Book of Forbes in the Miscellany of the Scottish History Society, Vol. 3, Second Series, 19, 224–321 (Edinburgh), 1919.

References

Alison, W.P.   1844   Remarks on the Report of Her Majesty's Commissioners on the Poor-Laws of Scotland, presented to Parliament in 1844, and on the Dissent of Mr. Twisleton from that Report, Edinburgh.

Cowan, I.B. & 1976   Medieval Religious Houses Scotland, London.
Easson, D.E.

Dallas, C. &   2002   Baconsthorpe Castle, Excavations and Finds, 1951-1972, East Anglian Archaeology Report 102, Norfolk.
Sherlock, D.

Firth Green, R. 2007   "Nede ne Hath no Lawe," Hanawalt, B. and Grotans, A., eds., Living Dangerously: On the Margins of Medieval and Early Modern Europe, Indiana, 9–30.

Haggarty, G.,   2011   "Sourcing Scottish Medieval Ceramics - the Use and Success of Chemical Analysis," in Proc. Soc. Antiq. Scot., 141, 249-267.
Hall, D. &
Jones, R.

Haggarty, G.   2017   "Medieval and Late Pottery", in Where There's Muck There's Money: The Excavation of Medieval and Post-Medieval Middens and Associated Tenement in Advocate's Close, Edinburgh, Engl, R, SAIR67, 16-34.

James, H.F.   2017   A Possible Almshouse at Creag a'Phuirt, Loch Lomond, Argyll & Bute, Scotland.

McAleese, R.   2012   "Aberdeen's Bedesmen - poverty and piety, Parts 1 and 2", in History Scotland, January/February 2012.

McConnochie, 1890   Bennachie, Aberdeen.
A.I.

Murdoch, K. R. 2008   "*Glass*", in The Bishop's Palace, Fetternear 2005-2006,
Dransart, P. & Trigg, J. (eds), 41-55, Lampeter:
Scottish Episcopal Palaces Project.
https://www.uwtsd.ac.uk/research/fetternear/
2005-2006-season/
https://www.researchgate.net/publication/273122298
_Scottish_Episcopal_Palaces_Project_the_bishop's
_palace_Fetternear_2005-2006

Nicholls, Sir G.1856   A History of the Scotch Poor Law in Connexion with
the Condition of the People, London.

Oliver, J.,   2013   *Historical Archaeology and the 'Colony': Reflections on*
Noble, G.,   *Fieldwork at a 19th-century Settlement in Rural Scotland",*
Shepherd, C.,   in Shepherd, C. (ed), Bennachie and the Garioch: Society
Knecht, R.,   and Ecology in the History of North-east Scotland,
Milek, K. and   Bennachie Landscapes Series: 2, 103-124.
Sveinbjarnarson, O.

Oliver, J.,   2016   *"The Bennachie Colony: A Nineteenth-Century Informal*
Armstrong, J.,   *Community in Northeast Scotland",* in International
Milek, K.,   Journal of Historical Archaeology, 20, 2, 341-377.
Schofield, J. Edward,
Gould, A. &
Noble, G.

Penny-Mason, 2014   *"The Children of the Reformation: Childhood*
B.J. &   *Palaeoepidemiology in Britain, AD 1000-1700",* in
Gowland, R.L.   Medieval Archaeology, 58, 162-194.

Phillips, E.   1720   The New World of English Words, or a General
Dictionary, 3rd edition, www.archive.org.

Shepherd, C.   2015   *"Changing Tenurial Forms and Renders in the North-east*
of Scotland between the Fifteenth and the Eighteenth
Centuries: Evidence of Social Development, Capitalised
Agrarianism and Ideological Change," in Rural History,
26, 1, 35-69.

Number 1

The Bennachie Colony Project:
Examining the Lives and Impact of the Bennachie Colonists
by Jennifer Fagen

On Traditional Rights on the Bennachie Commonty
The Beginning of the Colony
The Fight Between the Parishes
The Fate of the Colony

Number 2

Aerial Survey over Bennachie

Oral History at Bennachie

Discovering the Archives

Bringing the past to the present: Discoveries from the Archives

Flora and Fauna: The Natural History of Bennachie

The Forestry Commission's Acquisition of Bennachie

Keig School Community Cultural Heritage Project:
Interim Report on Archaeological Investigations

Oyne School Community Heritage Project: Oyne Through Time

Historical Archaeology and the 'Colony' on Bennachie

Number 3

The Geology Around Druminnor Castle

Flora and Fauna: A Study of Bennachie's Flora

A Short-lived Water-powered Mill at Keig: Interim Report

The 'English Quarry', Bennachie:
An Estimate of the Quantities of Granite Extracted and Exported

The Peatlands of Bennachie: An Introduction to Further Study

Division of the Commonty of 'Benachie': the 1858 Map

Excavations at Druminnor Castle, 2012 and 2013

Archaeology and the Bennachie Colony: Excavations of Two 19th Century Crofts

Pottery Finds from the Colony Site: Some Initial Observations

At the Back of Bennachie: A Nineteenth-century Rentier Farmstead?

THE BAILIES OF BENNACHIE

The Bailies of Bennachie

The Bailies of Bennachie

The Bailies of Bennachie

The Bailies of Bennachie